# Poilâne

# Poilâne

## Apollonia Poilâne

## THE SECRETS *of the* WORLD-FAMOUS BREAD BAKERY

*foreword by*
**ALICE WATERS**

*photographs by*
**Philippe Vaurès Santamaria**

A Rux Martin Book
**HOUGHTON MIFFLIN HARCOURT**
Boston New York 2019

Library of Congress Cataloging-in-Publication Data
is available.

ISBN: 978-1-328-81078-6 (hbk); 978-1-328-81082-3 (ebk)

Book design by Toni Tajima

Food and prop styling by Caroline Wietzel

Printed in China

C&C 10 9 8 7 6 5 4 3 2 1

*To you,*

*reader and wanderer, explorer of*
*the world of grains and fermentation.*

*Let's share bread!*

# Acknowledgments

THE SEEDS OF THIS BOOK were planted by my father and mother in my sister and me. They are seeds of passion, determination, and love for our crafts.

My sister, Athena, helped me germinate those seeds, and with the birth of her son, we now have another generation with whom to share our family story.

I'm so grateful to my baking mentors and guardian angels Alice Waters, Dorie Greenspan, and Ina Garten. Thank you for encouraging me to write this book and for providing guidance on how to cultivate my thoughts and ideas. My American adventure was brightened and smoothened by the guidance and professionalism of my book agent, Sarah Smith. Her guidance was key in helping me discover a new continent of publishing.

And, because one needs *copains* ("friends") in order to share bread, I thank all those who have contributed in some way to these pages. To my bakers and teams, to my testers, to my photographer, my stylist, and my designers, to my agent, to my editor and her team, I offer my sincere gratitude.

Thank you to Caroline Wietzel, Geneviève Brière-Godfrain, Guy Tatsinkou, Felix Fereira, Jean-François Aimé, Pascal Pauron, Philippe Vaurès Santamaria, Kate Wang, Mary Dodd, Rebekah Peppler, Rux Martin, Jamie Selzer, Melissa Lotfy, Toni Tajima, Judith Sutton, Sarah Kwak, Tian Mayimin, Martin Marquet, and Sudeep Rangi.

Although I have published several books in France, this is my first English-language project. I owe a special thank-you to Joanne Smart for collaborating with me. From our first meeting to our late-day (Paris time) phone calls, we shared a passion for food, and many moments of laughter and hardship to ensure that every page of this book reflects my thoughts and my bakery's philosophy, while being sensitive to an American audience.

# Contents

# Foreword

## A Story of Life and Bread

*by Alice Waters*

I FOUND POILÂNE ON RUE DU CHERCHE-MIDI IN PARIS IN 1971, and I can still picture that first loaf of bread I tasted: a big, beautiful round of *levain*, its crust a deep mahogany brown, with a complex, extraordinary flavor. Everything about it was unique, because, at the founding of the bakery in 1932, Apollonia's grandfather, Pierre Poilâne, had taken a traditional French bread and made it into something sublime. By the time I was tasting it, Apollonia's father, Lionel, was at the bakery's helm, and he understood the provenance of each of his ingredients. Lionel and his father before him knew the local farmers who grew the wheat for their stone-ground flour; they had perfected the proportions of salt, water, and flour, and they had determined the best kind of wood to use in the oven. There was a purity to each ingredient, and all the elements contributed to the delicious depth of flavor in the bread.

I believe that in many ways, all of the good bread we have now in the United States exists thanks to Poilâne's beautiful *miche*. I think about Steve Sullivan, for example, who worked at my restaurant, Chez Panisse, in the 1970s and later founded the legendary Acme Bread Company in Berkeley, California. Steve tasted Poilâne's bread on a summertime college trip to Europe in 1978, and after his return he was inspired to begin baking. This sort of transformative experience happened over and over and over again with bakers across the United States. Everything refers back to Poilâne.

One of the many things about Poilâne that I have always found admirable is the innovative method of production that Lionel created. The *Manufacture*, Lionel's baking hub outside of Paris, is what convinced me that it is, in fact, possible to create a larger business from a small one—that there is a way to scale up that feels true to the original. Poilâne has always maintained the purity of its ingredients and still embraces the charming irregularities that result when you dispose of the assembly-line model. At the *Manufacture*, teams of master bakers each produces their own loaves. Not every bread is identical—nor should they be!—because each is made by hand and the bakers follow their own instincts. You may not possess an ancient wood-fired oven, or Lionel's exact stone-ground wheat flour, or the Poilâne bread starter that has been lovingly tended since 1932—but with Apollonia's inspired recipe adjustments and a trust in your own bread-making instincts, you can arrive at a very faithful approximation of what you find at 8 rue du Cherche-Midi.

It has been a joy to watch the way in which Apollonia has so ably filled the shoes of her father and grandfather before her. She has had a preternatural poise and drive from the moment she assumed the mantle at the young age of eighteen. Even when she was running the bakery from her dormitory at Harvard, she was always tasting and perfecting and paying attention to the details, focusing on ingredients and elevating the bread to new heights. The bakery is her life's work.

When I visited Apollonia at the bakery recently and we descended into the basement bakehouse, it was like stepping back in time: There was the wood-fired oven just as it has been since 1932, the low curved ceiling above blackened from tens of thousands of bakes. Apollonia talked about listening to the faint crackling of the breads as they cool; well-baked loaves sing, she explained. Afterward, she took me up to a little workroom behind the shop where I ate sublime apple tarts (page 204) and toast underneath a curving chandelier made of bread, surrounded by 1930s artwork that Apollonia's grandfather had accepted as payment from artists who couldn't afford to pay for their loaves. Poilâne has always had a profound respect for tradition, and it is filled with remarkable talent and knowledge—and it is, above all, a deeply humane place.

What Apollonia shows us in these pages is that baking bread is truly a labor of love—born of time and repetition and the slow, patient reward that comes from tasting the results of your work. That reward grows over days, months, years, decades. In every recipe and story she shares, Apollonia reveals that baking means trusting all your senses: the feel of the dough in your hand, the distinctive tang of a starter you have nurtured, the door-knock resonance of a perfectly baked loaf when you rap on it. This symphony of the senses is what baking bread is about. It is about learning by doing. Poilâne and the Poilâne family have revolutionized the way we think about bread. And I can think of nothing more important than preserving and learning from that legacy.

# Introduction

A LITTLE AFTER 6 A.M., LATE AGAIN. I hurry into Poilâne, my family's flagship bakery in Paris, and race through the still-dark shop and down the stone steps, smooth and slippery from a perpetual dusting of flour and three centuries of use, to the basement bakehouse, all the while tucking rebellious strands of hair back into my bun. Fortunately for me, Felix, the master baker and my mentor, simply jokes about my tardiness. But beneath his light-hearted demeanor is a serious message: Because I'm late, I've missed the update on our bread production conveyed by the night baker.

In the fall of 2002, I had been apprenticing with Felix during high school holidays for two years. During the gap year I was taking between high school and Harvard, I was fully immersed in learning the craft of baking, working for six or seven hours at a time, days and nights.

There are no written recipes to follow at Poilâne. Our bakers are trained in a rigorous nine-month program during which they learn to bake using all their five senses. Although I was the owner's daughter, there were no shortcuts or cheat sheets for me. Like all the bakers, I would gradually get a feeling for the proper way to bake our breads and pastries through repetition and constant feedback from Felix. I wasn't used to the 500-degree heat of the wood-fired oven or strong enough to carry a five-pound basket of rising dough in each hand. I persevered because I had one goal: I, Apollonia Poilâne, would one day become the third generation to run this famous bakery. What I didn't know then—what none of us expected—was that the day would come much sooner than planned.

My grandfather, Pierre Poilâne, opened the bakery in 1932, when he was just twenty-three, at 8 rue du Cherche-Midi in the Saint-Germain-des-Prés district of Paris. The son of farmers from Normandy, he had wanted to be an architect, but his parents couldn't afford to send him to university. An interest in the mechanics of wood-fired ovens introduced him to baking, and he apprenticed in several *boulangeries* around France.

The building my grandfather chose for Poilâne had originally housed a convent before becoming a bakery at around the time of the French Revolution. He replaced the oven in the tunnel-like stone basement with one built to his own specifications. Although there were two other bakeries nearby, Poilâne stood out. Instead of making the popular white-flour baguettes, my grandfather drew inspiration from his childhood and returned to a kind of bread that had fallen out of favor after World War I: rugged hug-size loaves of sourdough with a deep flavor, slight acidity, tan interior from stone-ground flour, and a thick, crackly crust. And, rather than relying on commercial yeast, he made his own starter by mixing flour and water, harnessing the wild yeasts in the environment. That bread became the bakery's signature offering. Hearty and affordable, it was made to keep well, anchor a meal, and provide enough energy to get through a long day's work.

In the early 1930s, Saint-Germain-des-Prés was an up-and-coming neighborhood, a community of artists, many of them the starving variety. Locals came in daily for a whole loaf or, if they couldn't afford that, for a few slices that my grandfather sold by weight (something we still do). When an artist couldn't pay, my grandfather arranged a trade: bread for art—provided the paintings or drawings featured Poilâne in some way. Many line the walls of our offices today.

When my grandfather had to step back from the business in the early 1970s for health reasons, my father, Lionel, then in his mid-twenties, reluctantly stepped in. Having apprenticed in the bakery since he was fourteen, he knew the craft and family trade inside and out. Yet he loathed the idea, as he once put it, of being "trapped in this intellectual cupboard, this underground universe, completely removed from the outside life." So he figured out a solution. If he could not leave his oven to get out into the world, he would invite the world into his bakehouse. He saw bread as a main ingredient in the culture, politics, philosophy, and sensual experience of any civilized society, and he was eager to share that philosophy.

My father cut quite a figure. Elegant and handsome, with straight hair he grew almost to his chin, he favored bow ties (until my younger sister,

Athena, made him switch to regular ties) and the Nehru jackets in vogue in the 1970s. And he talked. A lot. Always with a smile, gesticulating nonstop. He befriended people from all of life's arenas, particularly artists—most famously, Salvador Dalí, who described my father as "the living Frenchman that I prefer." My father enjoyed reflective hobbies like fly-fishing and gardening, but he also had an adventurous streak. He became a licensed pilot and bought a helicopter, flying with my mother to their house on Île des Rimains off the coast of Brittany.

My father's passion for every aspect of bread—he amassed thousands of books on the subject—and his talent for communicating that passion enabled him to grow the public image of the bakery. Very quickly after taking over, he set his sights beyond the neighborhood and began developing a retail network, first domestically and then internationally.

The expanding business offered my mother, Irena—she went by IBU—an opportunity to use her artistic talents, and she worked with my father on designing everything from the look of the bakery to its packaging. A charismatic couple, they traveled the world together, sharing their love of our bread. With the combination of my father's outsize personality and my mother's formidable language skills—born in Poland, she moved to New York with her Ukrainian parents when she was thirteen—they attracted new customers as well as ample press. My father knew instinctively how to create excitement, collaborating with Dalí on bread-related sculptures. As a result, Poilâne's international reputation grew exponentially.

Faced with a growing demand that well exceeded the seventy-loaf capacity of the bakery's single oven, my father enlisted my mother, a trained architect, to design a building outside the city where he could continue my grandfather's artisanal baking methodology on a much larger scale. Together, my parents created a spectacular circular space housing twenty-four wood-burning ovens, which they called *La Manufacture Poilâne*. At the *Manufacture*, bakers could work in shifts around the clock to create thousands of loaves of our signature bread, all by hand. My father chose the name for its Latin roots: *manu factus* means "hand made." With the opening of the *Manufacture* in 1983, my father was able to supply restaurants and stores not only all over Paris but all over the world. To carry our bread became a badge of honor, and shops in France advertise it with signs proclaiming *"Ici, pain Poilâne"* ("Here, Poilâne bread"). Deliveries arrived regularly at Élysée Palace, the official residence of the president of France. These days, most of our air shipments go to the United States, to select markets and restaurants as well as the homes of fans. Our bread is also overnighted to places as far away as South Africa and Hong Kong.

In 2000, my father started thinking about opening a bakery outside France, and he set his sights on London. When it came time to ceremonially light the oven for the first time, my father asked my sister and me to do it. He believed there is something magical about lighting an oven; it is the promise of bread to come, but, even more, it is the transfer of fire—with its energy and light—to a new generation of bread and people. He had us stand in front of the oven, matchsticks in hand. Being adolescents, Athena and I could barely tolerate being made to pose, and we look sullen. But my father insisted we would one day be thankful to have the photo and, as was almost always the case, he was right.

At fifty-seven, my father was already starting to plan for his retirement. The intention was that after college, I would slowly begin taking over the reins of the company. As part of our grooming, our parents took my sister and me on field trips—literally. We visited fields of wheat in Beauce, a region in northern France known as the country's breadbasket, where my parents had contracted with farmers to grow wheat for us. My father also brought me with him to meetings or other business events. On weeknight bike rides through Paris, we would discuss his challenges and breakthroughs, and his ideas for growing the business.


Then, on October 31, 2002, everything changed. I was home alone that afternoon, having returned from my part-time job at the Gap, something I did to feel more like a normal teen. My parents had left earlier in the day to fly to our family home on Île-des-Rimains. When the phone rang, I assumed they were calling to let me know they arrived. Instead, it was one of my parents' friends. My father's helicopter had crashed into the sea off Brittany. Both my parents were killed. I was eighteen; Athena was sixteen.

The next day, I went to the bakery. I didn't rush down the stone steps into the warmth of the bakehouse, as I normally did. Instead, I slowly mounted the stairs to my father's office. I pulled his chair up to his desk and took his seat to continue the dream begun so long ago by my grandfather.

I went to college the next year and navigated class schedules and time zones to manage the bakery from my dorm. After a rocky and sleep-deprived start, I found my balance. My friends would come upon me pacing in Harvard Yard, fielding calls from France. To ensure quality control (and to make sure I started my day deliciously), I had bread overnighted to the college mailroom every Monday. As word caught on around campus, I started ordering extra bread to share with classmates. I kept my personal loaf in a jury-rigged breadbox fashioned from a thick cardboard box to help maintain the right level of hydration, and I took slices into the dining hall every morning for breakfast.

Each day, before heading to class, I called and checked on the bakery. Then, after homework and before bed, I would call Pascal, my master baker and production manager, and pummel him with questions. How did the quality of the loaves seem that night? How was the starter behaving? Did it need more water than usual? How are the new bakers doing with their training? Those calls kept me in tune with my bread and my team from afar. Every four to five weeks, I flew back to Paris for meetings that couldn't be done over the phone. Over breaks and summers, I went home to Paris, bringing along friends from school who toured the city while I worked at the bakery.

Although articles appeared profiling the college student running a world-famous bakery, my endeavor wasn't that remarkable at Harvard. Many of my fellow classmates were spending as much time on sports (one was a professional squash player), editing the *Harvard Crimson,* or launching their own companies, including Facebook. I returned to Paris in 2007 with a degree in economics and a desire to further expand the family's business.

Today we have a team of more than 200 men and women who bake and sell 5,000 loaves (and counting) of our breads and baked goods every day. And while I'm grateful for the tremendous support of my parents' friends and our longtime Poilâne staff, I can't say it's always been easy. There are moments when I would give anything to talk over an idea with my father. At such times, I find some solace in the continuity of what my grandfather created in 1932. His starter has spawned tens of thousands of loaves since then—and tens of thousands more to come.

This book tells the story of that darkly baked flour-dusted sourdough loaf engraved with a flour-dusted initial P. It's the story of how we managed to develop a worldwide business without compromising our craftmanship. It's also the story of where the bakery is heading. I explain how our bakers craft our famous loaves and show you how to make something similar at home. In addition, I share tips on how to store bread, how to bring out the best in it (see page 75 for a new way to make toast, for example), and how to use it in dishes from meatballs to ice cream. In the pages that follow, you will find the recipes for all the specialties. When I'm at our bakery, I am at home, and, with this book, I welcome you to it.

# About the Recipes

THESE RECIPES ARE SIMPLE. We don't go for fancy and fussy at Poilâne. But here are a few things to keep in mind to get the best results.

## USE HIGH-QUALITY INGREDIENTS

When a recipe contains just a few ingredients, it matters more that they are the best. For instance, we use a sea salt from Guérande in our bread. While you don't need to use the same salt, you do want to use one that tastes good, such as a French sea salt. Similarly, the flour we use in our breads is specially milled for us. When testing the recipes in the United States, we used King Arthur for all-purpose flour and whole wheat flours and Bob's Red Mill for flours from other grains, but feel free to use your own favorite high-quality brands.

The same goes for butter. European butters have a higher fat content and more flavor than most American butters and are worth seeking out. Otherwise, use the best American butter you can afford; we tested the recipes with Land O'Lakes. Note that these recipes use both unsalted (for most of the baking recipes) and salted butter.

All of this holds true for savory and main-course dishes as well: Ripe local tomatoes make all the difference in panzanella, and the ham and cheese you choose for your tartine determines whether your lunch is meh or magnificent.

## WEIGH INGREDIENTS, ESPECIALLY FLOUR

French bakers, even French home bakers, weigh ingredients rather than measure the amount by volume (cups and tablespoons). That is because volume measurements are less precise. A cup of flour measured by one person can be a greater or lesser amount than a cup measured by another, depending on whether they filled the cup with a light or heavy hand. (If you weigh your cup of flour regularly, you'll notice that your own cup measures can vary by as much as 10 to 20 grams.) A good scale is handy, but all of the recipes do include volume measures as well as weights if you don't have one. Also note that weights of flour are given first in metric because it's more precise.

## CONSIDER INVESTING IN A FEW TOOLS TO MAKE BREAD BAKING EASIER

If there is one must-have piece of equipment for making Poilâne's famous sourdough, it would be a 12-inch heavy-duty pot with a lid, such as a Dutch oven. Without it, you can't get the same dramatically large loaf. Some other pieces of equipment, though not as crucial, are nice to have, especially if you plan to make bread regularly. These include proofing baskets and a *lame* (a tool for scoring bread, although you can make do with a razor blade). But while these would definitely make your baking life easier, know that there are workarounds for all of these in the recipes.

Part One

# Morning

# BREADS and BREAKFAST

# Breads

Poilâne-Style Sourdough 50

WALNUT SOURDOUGH 52

Rye Bread 59

Rye Loaf with Currants 60

Black Pepper Pain de Mie 64

I USUALLY ARRIVE AT OUR CHERCHE-MIDI BOULANGERIE A LITTLE BEFORE IT OPENS AT 7:00 A.M. Though the street outside is quiet in the early morning light, the shop is already bustling. As the sales team carries trays of freshly baked breads and pastries up the stairs from the basement bakehouse to the shelves of our small storefront, the entire building fills with a rich, buttery aroma.

The golden, flaky croissants and *pains au chocolat* are carefully transferred to their place in the front window, the better to entice those who like to start their day with an indulgence. Loaves of our light, soft brioche also go in the window so that their glossy shine will catch the eyes of passersby.

Inside the store, our famously huge sourdough loaves are set up on their sides so that the giant P inscribed on top faces out. Breads featuring other grains, including wheat, rye, and corn, are placed on lower shelves within easy reach. A wicker basket filled with *punitions*, our beloved butter cookies, sits right by the cash register so our customers can take one (or two) to nibble on while they shop. By seven o'clock, a small crowd—students on their way to school, businessmen and -women, construction workers, local artists, and tourists—has lined up outside the glass front door. Once the door is unlocked, they pull on the wheat-shaped handle and enter the warm, fragrant bakery. Many are regulars who know exactly what they want. Others are first-time visitors who need a little more time to choose among the baked goods that literally surround them.

Customers often tell me they find the bakery simply by following their nose. I reply that I can tell the time of the day by the different aromas of breads and pastries coming out of the ovens. From the early morning, when the croissants emerge, browned, crisp, and irresistible, to the afternoon, when *pain de mie*, our sandwich bread, debuts, to the evening, when a new batch of sourdough is started, each hour has a distinctive smell.

So that the shelves of our store will be full when it opens, the bakehouse has been active since midnight. The night baker makes and shapes different doughs so they can be baked by Felix Fereira, our head baker. Felix begins his morning shift by conferring with the night baker. How has the dough been behaving? Is it rising fast or slow? How is the weather affecting it?

Before the night baker leaves, he and Felix lift a tarp-like cloth draped over a bathtub-size mixer. Together they smell and poke the starter that's left over from the previous batch, all the while discussing what it needs: more water, more flour, or more time. The two also check on the forty or so baskets holding rounds of dough, which the night baker shaped and left to rise. Stacked four to a layer, the baskets form a tower about five feet tall.

As Felix begins his baking, he moves from the mixer to the shaping table to the oven to the cooling racks with spare, precise actions honed by decades of working in the same small space. He wears running shoes, a white T-shirt—the better to hide the flour that lands everywhere—and, usually, linen shorts, because no matter the weather outside, the bakehouse is always warm. The wood-fired brick oven occupying the back wall, the one built by my grandfather when he opened the bakery in 1932, radiates constant heat. At 500°F, the oven, which can hold up to seventy loaves at one time, keeps the room a toasty 75°F to 80°F.

Shortly after he arrives, Felix checks on the fire underneath the baking chamber; he feeds it about every two hours. The still-warm ashes from the previous firing ignite the kindling he adds. The new wood takes a few minutes to catch, but when it does, it's like flipping a switch. The tips of its flames funnel up to the baking chamber through a plate-size hole in the oven floor. To funnel the heat to the back of the oven, Felix attaches a long steel pole to a cast-iron vent resembling a welder's helmet, called the *gueulard*, or "roaring mouth," and places it over the hole. Once the flames disappear, Felix removes the gueulard and inserts a bowl of water in its place to humidify the oven. There are no dials or gauges. Instead, Felix "reads" the temperature based on experience. Some of the other bakers, especially those new to Poilâne, may estimate the heat by placing a piece of paper in it for a few seconds; they can determine its intensity by observing the color change.

With the oven stoked and the shaped dough rising, Felix moves on to making the next batch. Singing along to the pop music playing on his radio, he turns from the oven to the mixer containing the starter. From a shaft over the mixing bowl, he releases a stream of flour from the storage room a flight above that holds the vast supply required daily. He adds water from a nearby spigot and salt by the cupful, relying not on precise measures but on his knowledge of what the dough needs. Once the dough is mixed, Felix transfers it—all one hundred sixty or so pounds of it—piece by piece to a trough-like wooden bin, where it will rest before being shaped. The dough is left to rest, but Felix's work has just begun: It's time to bake the loaves left by the night baker. He grabs one of the long-handled wooden *pelles* ("peels") suspended from a rack over his head near the mouth of the oven, flips two of the loaves onto it, swiftly but meticulously slashes the tops with our signature P, and slides the loaves off the peel toward the back of the oven. He will repeat these actions another twenty or so times before closing the cast-iron door.

Meanwhile, in an adjacent room, two or three pastry chefs are at work making cookies and pastries, including croissants, pains au chocolat, and tarts. Thanks to the thick door and the massive refrigerator built into the pastry room's far wall, it's much cooler in there, perfect for handling buttery doughs.

Once the pastries are shaped, one of the chefs wheels a rack loaded with them into the bakehouse. Felix deftly transfers the baking sheets of pastries to the oven. Since they will bake much more quickly than the bread, Felix returns to the oven repeatedly, using the peel to move the sheets around for even cooking. Then he transfers the breads and pastries to cooling racks.

In between baking, Felix returns his attention to the sourdough he made earlier. He sets proofing baskets down on the long table between the mixer and the oven and flours the table well. He quickly portions the dough, weighing each piece on a hanging scale (because he's been doing this for so long, he almost never needs to adjust the amount of dough). It takes him about three seconds to shape a loaf: He rolls the piece of dough over right to left and then, with two hands, flips it bottom over top to form a round. Cupping his hands around the dough, he turns it to create a taut ball and then flips the ball into one of the waiting baskets. Watching him work is to see a master in action, each movement a reflection of his skill and experience.

Throughout the remainder of the morning, work continues like a well-orchestrated ballet, breads and pastries continuously moving in and out of the oven before being whisked up the stairs to be sold. Over the years, I've come to recognize the stages of baking from the rhythmic sounds emanating from the bakehouse: the whoosh and crackling of the wood-fired oven as it heats; the loud hum of the stand mixer kneading the dough; the slight spring of the scale as our bakers cut and weigh the dough; the scrape of the wooden peel on the oven floor; the symphony of crusts crackling as they release steam when cooling. These sounds serve as my clock. It's a delightful way to tell time. Felix's shift ends around noon, but he won't leave until the next baker arrives so that he can report on how the sourdough is behaving that day, to help ensure consistency.

Felix Fereira, the master baker,
at the bakehouse at Rue de Cherche-Midi

# SOURDOUGH AT POILÂNE

THE RECIPES IN THIS BOOK BEGIN THE SAME WAY POILÂNE STARTED: WITH SOURDOUGH. At first sight, our round, four-pound loaf is striking. If you've not seen one and want to get a sense of its generous dimensions, put your arms out in front of you, then connect your fingers to form a circle; that's about the diameter. Now imagine a dark, crackling, chocolate-brown crust; a tantalizing, fresh-baked aroma; and a tan, chewy, slightly tart crumb inside.

The word *sourdough* refers both to the bread and to the starter, a ferment used in place of packaged yeast. At its most basic, a sourdough starter is made with flour combined with warm water. As the mixture sits, friendly bacteria, as well as the wild yeasts living on flour and in the bakehouse, work together via fermentation to make the bread rise and give it a complex, rich, slightly tangy flavor. Our sourdough is kept alive by reserving a piece of dough from each batch to serve as a starter for the next.

Any sourdough loaf is affected not only by the environment in which it is made but also by the ingredients used, the weather, and the methods and habits of the baker. Poilâne's distinctive sourdough dates, quite literally, back to my grandfather's first batch in 1932. Since his very first loaves, a piece of each batch of dough has been kept to act as the starter for the next batch, meaning there's a bit of 1932 in today's bread. The recipe we use today in the bakehouse, which is made with just flour, water, and salt, is also the same one he used.

The process starts, aptly, with the starter. (This piece of dough can also be called *la mère,* meaning "mother dough.") By adding water and flour to la mère and letting it rest, you get sourdough, or dough gone sour through fermentation. To make the actual bread, more flour, salt, and water are added to the starter.

People often mistakenly think our sourdough is made with whole wheat because of its tan crumb. The color, however, comes from our flour, which includes about 15 percent of the wheat bran. In France, this is what we would call T80 flour in a classification system that's based on ash content, which refers to the mineral composition of the wheat bran. There are six most commonly used types, with Type 45 (T45) being the whitest (not unlike the Italian 00 used to make fresh pasta) and T150 the darkest. But not all T80 flours, the kind we use, have the same flavor and characteristics. Our flour, which is entirely stone-milled for us from a blend of carefully selected wheat varieties that can vary from year to year, plays an important role in the unique flavor, texture, and color of our sourdough.

For the salt, we use Guérande sea salt. This famous salt, hand-harvested in Brittany, is unrefined and free of additives; due to its unique terroir, it has a soft, rich flavor that is distinct enough that when, about fifteen years ago, we had to replace it temporarily (due to an oil spill in an adjacent region), many of our customers said they could taste the difference in the bread!

The only other ingredient is water. Many bakers talk about mineral levels of water and what effects they can have on the final product. But what matters more to us is the amount of water. A wetter dough is less stiff, allowing the air bubbles in the dough to expand more. More hydrated sourdoughs have a dark crust like ours but, when sliced, reveal a very open crumb. Our dough is not overly hydrated, so a Poilâne miche has a more dense, even crumb that makes fantastic toast and a superb base for tartines. It's not that one style is better or worse, but we take great pride in our chewy sourdough, with its rich flavor that seems to only improve a day or two after baking.

Once the ingredients are mixed, the baker transfers the dough by hand to *la pâtière*, a coffee-table-size wooden box that, used batch after batch, has developed an environment that fosters fermentation. Even when empty, the box has a slightly sour aroma, not unlike that of a light beer or a soft dry cheese, from the fermentation that regularly goes on within. The baker transfers pieces of the dough, each one roughly about the size of a loaf of bread, one at a time to la pâtière. This allows him to judge the quality and resistance of each piece as it's placed in the box. Then the dough is covered and allowed to rest for about two hours.

After this rest, the baker cuts the dough into smaller pieces, weighing each one to make sure that it weighs 2.3 kilograms (about 5 pounds). Most of our bakers can weigh a loaf just by eye and feel and use the scale simply for quality control; out of one hundred loaves, a good baker may have to adjust the size of just one or two. After he has weighed out a half dozen or so pieces, the baker shapes each one into a round. Watching an experienced baker at work, swiftly executing these precise, repetitive steps, is almost hypnotizing. After shaping, he flips the loaf over into a waiting floured wicker basket so that the top (smooth) side faces down. With one glance at the dough in the basket, I can gauge the shaping skill of the baker. The bottom of a loaf made by an inexperienced baker can resemble a crater; his rolling and folding did not adequately bring the sides of the dough together. When it has been shaped by a veteran baker, however, the sides of the folded dough form a small neat line called a *clé* ("key"). The loaves proof in these baskets for a couple hours before baking.

When it's time to bake, the baker carefully flips the loaves onto the end of a wooden peel big enough to hold two loaves. Just before the loaves go in the oven—indeed as they sit at the mouth of the oven on the peel—the baker uses a lame (LAHM) to score each loaf with a cursive P. Although the P, which stands both for our last name as well as *pain* (the French word for "bread"), has a standardized style, each baker's "handwriting" is different, so each P is unique.

The scored loaves are immediately transferred to the wood-fired oven and baked until they are a deep brown, about an hour. Practiced bakers can usually tell just by looking at a loaf whether it's properly baked, but they also test by knocking hard on the bottom of the loaf; if it sounds like a knock on a wooden door, the loaf is done.

The final step in the baking process actually happens after the loaves come out of the oven. Using gloves to handle the very hot loaves, the bakers stand the loaves on their sides on cooling racks, nestled next to each other like books on a shelf. This proximity is vital for a crisp crust. As the bread cools, any moisture inside will travel outward from the interior to escape. The proximity of the loaves means excess steam will be reabsorbed instead of condensing on the crusts. The crackling sounds the loaves make as they cool are a faint but beautiful melody.

# TIPS FOR MAKING THE POILÂNE-STYLE SOURDOUGH

## WEIGH THE INGREDIENTS, BUT TRUST YOUR INSTINCTS—AND TAKE NOTES.

When it comes to measuring ingredients, it's best to rely on weight, but it's important to trust your instincts and your experience as well. Sometimes your dough may need a little more water; other times, a little more flour. Take notes when you make bread, marking down the time of day, the weather, and the temperature in the kitchen. Include your impression of the dough. And after the bread has baked, note its density, the thickness of the crust, and the flavor. Over time, you may notice patterns that will help you adjust as necessary to create consistent results. Note, however, that when making adjustments, the amount of an ingredient you add should not exceed 10 percent of the original quantity.

- In a warm, dry environment, doughs tend to "drink" more. If you notice your dough is a bit dry, add more water.

- In a humid environment, doughs retain more liquid and may be sticky. In that case, add a dusting of flour.

- The optimal temperature for mixing and proofing sourdough is one where you feel warm enough to work while wearing a T-shirt: 68°F to 77°F (20°C to 25°C). If your kitchen is too warm, the dough will rise too quickly, which can cause the bread to collapse during baking. If, on the other hand, the room is too cool and the dough is not given more time to rise, the bread will be dense. Adjust the timing or let the dough rise in a warmer spot.

## BEGIN WITH A STARTER.

Breads made with a starter—also known as a pre-ferment, levain, or mother dough—tend to have more flavor, better texture, and longer shelf life than those leavened with commercial yeast alone. A sourdough starter is created by mixing flour and water and allowing the airborne wild yeasts and (good) bacteria that live on the flour to thrive and multiply. As the starter begins to ferment, the yeasts feed on the sugars in the flour, converting the carbohydrates to bubbles of water and carbon dioxide, which both expand the dough during the proofing period and create the characteristic tang.

The sourdough recipe on page 50 uses two fermentations. The first is a simple combination of yogurt, water, salt, and time that serves to kick-start the process. After twenty-four hours, the first fermentation is "fed" with flour and water, giving it more sugars to continue to convert and solidifying the base of the sourdough loaf's flavor. After another twenty-four hours, the starter is ready to use.

You may wonder why I suggest making a starter with yogurt, something my grandfather never would have dreamed of doing. The reason is that yogurt, because it's a fermented product, fosters fermentation and helps the dough achieve a balanced acidity. It is particularly useful if you're not working in a bakehouse like Poilâne, where the constant cycle of bread production provides our breads with an immersive boost in fermentation from the very beginning.

Maintaining a sourdough starter is like having a pet. You need to feed it (with water and flour) and pamper it (in a warm, draft-free space) to keep it healthy and happy for making batches of bread. At Poilâne, we bake bread every day, so the starter is continuously fed and fermented with each new batch of bread. If you bake bread every day, you can do the same, but since that's unlikely, you'll need to set up a schedule to feed your starter (see page 51). The daily ritual of maintaining your starter can be a chore (you'll need to find someone to tend to it when you go on vacation!), but the reward is in the bread that results. Over time, your starter will develop its own personality and unique flavors, based on your ingredients, environment, and care.

### MIX BY HAND.

I strongly suggest mixing your sourdough by hand to literally get a feel for it from start to finish. If you do use a mixer, stop it occasionally and check the dough for elasticity: Generously flour one hand and, using all your fingers, gently pinch the dough and pull some away. The dough should follow your movement and then retract nicely when let go. If it tears or breaks, it needs more water; if it's too sticky, add some more flour and mix until combined.

### SHAPE A TAUT ROUND.

Shaping is the part of the process that requires the most practice. To shape the dough, lightly flour your work surface; you don't want to use too much flour—the dough should stick a little. Transfer the dough from the bowl to the work surface. Roll it from right to left to create a smooth top while forming an even round. When the top feels nice and taut, gently place the dough in the basket, smooth side down.

### PROOF THE DOUGH IN A BASKET OR COLANDER.

For the final stage of fermentation, we cradle our loaves in generously floured linen-lined wicker baskets to give them their shape. If you don't have a proofing basket, you can line a large colander with a linen cloth and generously flour it; the colander's holes mimic the basket's weave. Flouring the linen serves several purposes: First, the dough is less likely to stick when you are ready to unmold it for baking. Second, the cloth absorbs excess moisture, leaving (once you've inverted the dough for baking) a clean top that makes the loaf easier to score, and the flour left on the dough makes the scored design pop more.

At Poilâne, we don't wash our cloths between batches of bread because the flour actually fosters fermentation. This can affect proofing time: In the sourdough recipe on page 50, I give proofing times for a clean new cloth. After making your first batch of dough, don't wash your cloth—simply give it a shake before storing it in a plastic bag. For your next batch, expect proofing to take 10 to 15 percent less time, as long as other variables, such as temperature, stay relatively the same. When too much flour has accumulated, simply use a bench scraper (aka pastry cutter) to scrape most of it off.

### SCORE THE DOUGH TO CONTROL EXPANSION.

Scoring the dough—slashing its top with a lame or razor blade just before baking—isn't just for decoration; it helps control the expansion of the loaf during baking and directs the cracking that would otherwise occur naturally. How deep to score the dough depends on how the dough proofed. If your loaf is properly proofed, apply about the same pressure you would use to write on a piece of paper with a pen. If your loaf is a little underproofed and could use a boost in the oven, score it more deeply. If your dough is too supple or has overproofed, score lightly, barely marking it (in this case, the scoring is mainly for looks and has little to do with expansion).

With its curved double-sided blade and handle, a lame makes scoring easy. You can score whatever design you like into the top of your loaf. If you would like to try your hand at our signature P, hold the lame like a pen. Starting about one-third of the way down from the top of the loaf, score the bottom half of a swirly capital S. Score a large arch to resemble a cursive P over the top. But no matter how you score the loaf, do it with confidence; if you hesitate, the blade can catch and rip the dough instead of making a nice, neat cut. As with most things concerning bread baking, the more you do it, the better you will become.

### BAKE THE LOAF COMPLETELY.

At Poilâne, where we bake in wood-fired brick-lined ovens, we add moisture as needed via a cast-iron pot of water that is suspended above the flames. To mimic that heat and humidity, bake the bread in a preheated heavy stew pot and keep it covered for the first ten minutes of baking. During this initial period, the moisture that escapes from the dough is trapped in the pot, creating steam. The moisture in the pot keeps the top of the loaf supple, allowing for maximum expansion during those first ten minutes of baking. It also dissolves sugars on the surface of the dough, which then bake to form a deeply flavorful, crackly crust.

A well-baked sourdough loaf will have a dark-brown crust. To determine if it's cooked through, remove the pot from the oven and, using oven mitts, take the bread out of the pot, set it on one side, and knock on the bottom; you should hear a clear sound like a knock on a wooden door. You can also tell that your bread is close to done when you can smell it. One night while testing recipes, I fell asleep with bread in the oven and woke up to the smell. The loaf was on the darker side but still delicious.

### LET THE LOAF COOL BEFORE SLICING.

Bread hot from the oven is so alluring you'll want to break right into it, but try to be patient. The inside continues to bake as the loaf cools, so give it some time, or it may be gummy. The best way to cool bread is to transfer it to a rack, so air can circulate around it, cover it with a thick cloth, and let it sit for at least an hour. The cloth will absorb excess moisture as the loaf cools, ensuring slices that don't stick to each other when cut. For how to slice and store your bread, see pages 177 and 178.

# Poilâne-Style Sourdough

This recipe produces a loaf similar to our sourdough, with a chewy, sweet-sour crumb and a chocolate-brown crust that crackles when sliced. After many tests in the home kitchen, I was finally able to duplicate the elusive balance of acidity and sweetness in our bread that is known as *suret*. The slices are just as good plain as they are toasted with butter and jam.

The first time you make this bread, you will need to begin by making the starter, in this case a mix of yogurt, water, and flour. Left to sit, the mixture will begin to ferment. Then the dough sits again to ferment once more, and this second fermentation gives the loaf additional flavor and helps it to expand in the oven. If you've made sourdough before, you may be used to a bubbly, liquidy starter; this one is firm and more like the piece-of-dough starter we use at the bakery.

Once you have the starter going, it's an easy task to use it to make batch after batch of bread. I offer tips for getting the best results, but if you are a novice baker, don't worry if your bread isn't perfect on the first try; it may take some practice before the movements of mixing, shaping, and scoring feel natural. The instructions here are fairly basic; if you are new to bread baking and want more direction, see page 47.

MAKES ONE 12-INCH (30-CM) ROUND LOAF

**FOR THE STARTER**

*First fermentation*

⅔ cup (160 ml) lukewarm (100°F to 110°F; 37°C to 43°C) water

¼ cup (60 g) plain whole-milk yogurt (regular or Greek-style; be sure the label specifies "live active cultures")

150 g (1 cup plus 1 tablespoon) all-purpose flour

60 g (⅓ cup plus 2 tablespoons) whole wheat flour

*Second fermentation*

140 g (1 cup) all-purpose flour

60 g (⅓ cup plus 2 tablespoons) whole wheat flour

⅓ cup (80 ml) lukewarm (100°F to 110°F; 37°C to 43°C) water

The mixture from the first fermentation

**FOR THE BREAD**

410 g (all but 1 cup) of the mixture from the second fermentation

550 g (4 cups) all-purpose flour, plus more for dusting

450 g (3¼ cups) whole wheat flour

1½ teaspoons (4 g) active dry yeast

2¾ cups (650 ml) lukewarm (100°F to 110°F; 37°C to 43°C) water

1 tablespoon (20 g) fine sea salt

**MAKE THE FIRST FERMENTATION:** In a medium bowl, whisk the water and yogurt until combined. Add both flours and mix until the dough starts to come together. (The mixture should feel a little like chewed gum.) Cover loosely with a kitchen towel and set aside in a warm (72°F to 77°F/22°C to 25°C), draft-free place for 24 hours.

**MAKE THE SECOND FERMENTATION:** Add both flours and the water to the bowl with the first fermentation and mix together with your hands (flour your hands first to keep from sticking). Once the mixture starts coming together, transfer to a clean work surface and use a dough scraper to continue to scrape up and mix the starter until thoroughly combined; it should still be quite sticky. Gently stretch two opposite sides of the mixture and fold into the center, then repeat with the other two sides to create a ball. Return to the bowl, cover with the kitchen towel, and set aside in a warm, draft-free place for another 24 hours. The mixture won't change much in appearance, but you should see some bubbles, and the top will look a little wet. At this point, the starter is ready to use.

**FEEDING THE STARTER:** If you are not ready to bake bread the day the starter is ready, you will need to feed it. Every day (or every other day) that you don't use your starter, divide it in half, discarding half (or give it to a friend). To the remaining starter, add 140 g (1 cup) all-purpose flour, 56 g (½ cup) whole wheat flour, and ½ cup plus 1½ tablespoons (150 ml) water and mix until combined. Cover the starter loosely with plastic wrap, cover the bowl with a kitchen towel, and refrigerate for another 24 hours before using. (You can store and feed the starter this way indefinitely.)

**MAKE THE BREAD:** Transfer the 410 g (all but 1 cup) starter to a large bowl (see Note on page 52 for what to do with the rest). Add both flours and the yeast. Combine the water and salt, stir to dissolve the salt, and add to the bowl. Using your hands, mix until combined. Transfer the dough to a lightly floured clean surface and knead until it comes together in a homogeneous mass and feels smooth, 10 to 15 minutes.

Return the dough to the bowl, cover the bowl with a clean kitchen towel, and set aside in a warm, draft-free place for about 45 minutes. The dough should increase in volume by 150 to 200 percent, though you're not looking for volume as much as a gentle expansion and increased resistance. To test, use the back of your hand to gently touch the surface of the dough; you should feel a slight resistance that's just strong enough so the dough returns to its shape.

*Very generously* flour a 12- to 14-inch (30- to 35.5-cm) linen-lined proofing basket, being sure to get the flour on the sides of the basket as well. Alternatively, line a large metal colander with a linen cloth and very generously flour that. Lightly flour the work surface.

Transfer the dough to the work surface and, using your hands, very gently flatten it to two-thirds its original size. Roll the dough over from right to left, then tuck the sides of the dough under while rotating the dough on the work surface to create a nice round with a taut top. Turn the dough over and place it smooth side down in the prepared basket. Cover with the kitchen cloth and set in a warm, draft-free place.

After 2 hours, check on the dough: You're looking for it to expand and gain resistance. To test, touch the dough lightly with the back of your hand; if

continued

it maintains its shape, it's ready. If it isn't, proof for 5 to 10 more minutes in a warmer space (such as your stovetop while the oven is heating). Conversely, if the dough deflates immediately when you touch it, it has overproofed, and you should bake it immediately.

Meanwhile, about 25 minutes before baking, position a rack in the lower third of the oven, place a 12-inch (30-cm) ovenproof pot such as a Dutch oven on it, and preheat to 475°F (245°C).

Using oven mitts, remove the pot from the oven. With one swift movement, being mindful of the hot sides of the pot, flip the dough into the pot so its smooth side faces up. Use a lame (or razor blade) to quickly score the dough; you can score a square shape, a hashtag, a cursive P (as at Poilâne), or any other design you like. Cover the pot and bake for 10 minutes. Remove the lid and continue baking until the crust is dark brown and caramelized, another 45 minutes to 1 hour.

Using oven mitts, carefully turn the loaf out of the pot and check it for doneness: Stand the loaf on its side and knock on the bottom; it should sound like you're knocking on a door. If it doesn't, continue to bake directly on the oven rack, checking every 5 minutes or so, until it sounds hollow when tapped. Place the baked loaf on a wire rack, cover with a thick clean cloth, and let cool for at least 1 hour before slicing.

Stored in a paper bag or wrapped in linen at room temperature, the loaf will keep for up to 1 week.

**NOTE:** You can make a starter from the leftover second fermentation—you will have about 240 g (1 cup)—by mixing in 90 g (⅔ cup) all-purpose flour, 40 g (a heaping ¼ cup) whole wheat flour, and ⅓ cup (80 ml) water. Let sit for 24 hours before using. If not using the starter within 1 day, maintain the starter as directed on page 51.

## Variation

### WALNUT SOURDOUGH

We make smaller loaves of sourdough with walnuts, and it's one of our most popular breads. Chop 2 cups (240 g) toasted walnuts and knead into the bread dough. After the first rise, divide the dough into 6 pieces. Proof and then bake the loaves on a baking sheet at 475°F until the crust is dark brown, 35 to 45 minutes. You can use the bread for Baked Camembert Casse-Croûte (page 160).

# DECORATING BREAD

DECORATING A LOAF OF BREAD IN BAS-RELIEF WITH, SAY, SHEAVES OF WHEAT, IS A VENERABLE FRENCH TRADITION. After my grandfather opened Poilâne, he would embellish his loaves with a cluster of grapes for the celebration of the wine harvest or with an elaborate bouquet of bread flowers for a wedding. My parents made place cards for dinner parties by "writing" a person's name in dough and baking it.

At the bakery, we regularly offer decorated loaves themed to the calendar. February, for example, gets a cluster of hearts; July has a bouquet of wheat to celebrate the harvest; and August showcases seashells and sea stars as a nod to the summer holidays. As an homage to my American side, I also make Thanksgiving breads decorated with a turkey. And, inspired by my travels to Japan, I've created loaves topped with cherry blossoms. Our customers often ask us to decorate a bread for a special occasion—a great conversation-starter at the table. Each order further fosters the bond between our customers and us, as well as the relationship between art, bread, and community. While these bread decorations will keep for a long time, they, like all of us, will eventually turn to dust, a transience I find beautiful.

The bakers at Poilâne are true artists, and each has a distinctive style. But decorating with dough is something you can easily do at home. To start, you will need to add additional flour to a sourdough starter or dough so that it will hold its shape and bake harder than the loaf itself. Then, with a little practice, you can make your own roses, leaves, letters, or other creations to customize your loaf. These will keep for a long time—they are too dense to eat.

continued

## TO MAKE THE DECORATIVE DOUGH

In the bowl of a stand mixer fitted with the paddle attachment, add all-purpose flour a little at a time to the sourdough starter (page 50) or a piece of sourdough bread dough (page 51) until it can take no more. (Alternatively, mix the flour into the dough with a sturdy wooden spoon.) Knead until a very thick, pliable dough forms. Keep the dough covered with plastic wrap until ready to use.

## TO MAKE A ROSE

Roll the dough into a ⅛-inch (⅓-cm)-thick rectangle. Cut out five 1½-inch (3.75-cm) circles. Using a pastry brush, brush one circle with a little water, then use your fingers to gently pinch the circle until it's paper-thin. Roll up the circle at a bit of an angle to create a spiral cone; this is the center of your flower. Then build your rose, one petal at a time. Brush another circle with water and pinch until very thin. Shape this "petal" around the rose's center, gently pressing it into place, then pull back the top edge to give it dimension and shape. Repeat with another circle, placing this petal opposite the second and being sure to keep the petals aligned at the top; if the petals start turning downward, you'll have something that looks more like a pinecone. Repeat with the remaining circles. Five circles will create a rosebud. To make a rose in bloom, roll out more dough and cut more circles; you will need 6 or 7. Using scissors, cut off the excess dough at the bottom of the rose to create a flat base so it can stand upright. Repeat to make more roses, if you like.

## TO MAKE LEAVES

If you would like to add leaves to your rose, roll out more dough and cut out 2 or 3 leaf shapes with a leaf-shaped cutter or a paring knife. Using the dull back of the knife, press lines into the dough to make veins. Lightly brush the bottom of a leaf with a little water and attach it to the base of the finished rose; repeat with the remaining leaves. You can also use leaves on their own as decoration.

## TO MAKE A BANNER AND LETTERS

You will need 2 pieces of dough, one for the banner and one for the letters. For the banner, roll out a thin rectangle that's 6 inches (15 cm) long by 1 inch (2.5 cm) high. If you like, cut a triangle from the middle of each end to make it look more like a banner. Cover with plastic wrap. For the letters, roll the remaining dough into a thin rope and shape it into letters. Moisten the back of each to help them stick. Brush the banner lightly with water so the letters will adhere. Press the letters lightly onto the banner.

## TO BAKE THE DECORATIONS

Preheat the oven to 400°F (200°C).

*If the decorations will stand on their own*: Line a baking sheet with parchment paper. Using a pastry brush, brush the decorations lightly with water and place on the baking sheet. Bake until the decorations are browned and set, about 30 minutes.

*If attaching your decorations to a loaf of bread*: Bake the bread for about one-third of its baking time. Moisten both the bread and the decorations with water, attach the decorations to the loaf, and finish baking it.

# Rye Bread

While Americans tend to think of rye bread as a longish loaf studded with caraway seeds, that's not the style we make. Ours uses a sourdough starter and a special rye flour to create a hearty loaf with a slight floral scent and a rustic flavor, with notes of honey and toasted grains and a pleasant chocolaty-malt aftertaste.

MAKES ONE 9-INCH (23-CM) ROUND LOAF

230 g (1¼ cups) starter from Poilâne-Style Sourdough (page 50)

435 g (3 cups plus 2 tablespoons) rye flour

¾ teaspoon (2 g) active dry yeast

1½ cups (360 ml) water

1½ teaspoons (9 g) fine sea salt

All-purpose flour, for dusting

Put the starter in a large bowl. Add the rye flour and yeast. In a small bowl, combine the water and salt, stir to dissolve the salt, and add to the flour mixture. With wet hands, mix and knead the dough in the bowl until it comes together in a smooth, homogeneous mass.

Transfer the dough to a work surface and shape it into a ball. Return it to the bowl, cover with a cloth, and let rest for 15 minutes.

Reshape the dough into a round, return it to the bowl, cover, and let rise in a warm (72°F to 77°F/22°C to 25°C), draft-free place for 1½ hours.

While the dough is rising, generously flour a 9-inch (23-cm) linen-lined proofing basket. Or line a similar-size colander with a linen cloth and very generously flour that.

Using wet hands, shape the dough into a ball and place it in the basket or colander.

Let rise in a warm, draft-free place until it doubles in size, about 1½ hours.

Meanwhile, about 25 minutes before baking, position a rack in the lower third and preheat the oven to 475°F (245°C). Line a baking sheet with a Silpat liner or parchment paper.

Transfer the dough to the prepared baking sheet. Use a lame (or a razor blade or sharp paring knife) to quickly score the dough (we score a square). Bake for 45 minutes. Carefully remove the loaf from the oven and check it for doneness by standing the loaf on its side and knocking on the bottom; it should sound like you're knocking on a door. If it doesn't, bake for 5 minutes more and check again. Transfer the baked loaf to a wire rack and let cool for 2 hours before slicing.

Stored in a paper bag or wrapped in linen at room temperature, the bread will keep for up to 1 week.

---

NOTE: As with our sourdough, you will either need to have the starter on hand or plan ahead to make it, which takes a couple of days.

# Rye Loaf with Currants

My father regularly ran home from the bakery before we went to school to drop off a small version of this loaf for our morning snack. He would cut it in half, add a generous pat of butter, and pack it for us to enjoy in his car. Today I still love to have a few slices—buttered or not—for breakfast or as a midmorning treat.

We make this in metal loaf pans, but you can also shape it freeform.

MAKES ONE 9-BY-5-INCH (23-BY-13-CM) LOAF

1½ cups (240 g) dried currants

2½ cups (595 ml) hot water

230 g (1¼ cups) starter from Poilâne-Style Sourdough (page 50)

435 g (3 cups plus 2 tablespoons) rye flour

¾ teaspoon (2 g) active dry yeast

1½ teaspoons (9 g) fine sea salt

Neutral oil, such as canola or sunflower seed, for the pan

Put the currants in a medium bowl, add the hot water, and let soak for 10 minutes.

Set a fine-mesh sieve over a bowl and drain the currants; reserve the soaking liquid. Pat the currants dry with a paper towel and reserve.

Put the starter in a large bowl. Add the rye flour and yeast. In a small bowl, combine 1½ cups (355 ml) of the reserved soaking liquid (save the rest for brushing the loaf) and the salt, stir to dissolve the salt, and add to the flour mixture, along with the currants. With wet hands, mix and knead the dough in the bowl until it comes together in a smooth, homogeneous mass. Transfer the dough to a work surface and shape into a ball. Return it to the bowl and let rest for 15 minutes.

Reshape the dough into a round, return to the bowl, cover with a cloth, and let rise for 1½ hours.

Brush a 9-by-5-inch (23-by-13-cm) pan with oil. Turn the dough out and, using wet hands to prevent sticking, shape it into a 9-by-4-inch (23-by-10-cm) log. Transfer to the oiled pan. Brush a piece of plastic wrap with oil, drape it over the loaf, and let it rise in a warm (72°F to 77°F/22°C to 25°C), draft-free place until it rises about ½ inch (1.25 cm) above the sides of the pan, 1½ to 2 hours.

Meanwhile, about 25 minutes before baking, position a rack in the lower third and preheat the oven to 450°F (230°C).

Use a pastry brush to brush the top of the loaf with the reserved currant-soaking liquid. Bake until the loaf is golden and firm, 45 to 50 minutes; if you carefully remove it from the pan, it should feel hollow when you knock on it. Transfer the pan to a wire rack and let cool for 1 hour.

Remove the loaf from the pan, return to the rack, and let cool completely before slicing. Stored in a paper bag or wrapped in linen at room temperature, the loaf will keep for up to 1 week.

---

NOTE: As with our sourdough, you will either need to have the starter on hand or plan ahead to make it, which takes a couple of days.

# BAKING WITH ALL YOUR SENSES

At Poilâne, it takes nine months to train a baker. Each apprentice is paired with a master who demonstrates his daily routine one step, sometimes even one motion, at a time. On the first day of training, the apprentice observes and the master bakes; by the last day, they have reversed roles. We choose our master bakers based on their skill and experience, but we also look for the willingness and joy they take in sharing their knowledge.

During months of training, our masters show the novices how to vary the amounts of flour and water as necessary, depending on the grain and when it was harvested. They school them in how to feel the dough, stopping the mixer to make sure the gluten is developing properly. They teach them how the rise determines the final texture of the bread and how to adjust the fire so that each loaf is perfectly done.

Your five senses will ensure quality and consistency in your loaves.

## TOUCH

Your hands not only shape the dough but also gauge its texture, resistance, and temperature. A baker's touch should be assured yet gentle enough to avoid breaking the gluten strands that trap the carbon dioxide, which is essential for rising. Practicing quick, confident movements is key to becoming a good baker.

## SMELL

Your sense of smell is second only to touch in determining when the dough is ready to be baked. Look for a noticeable yet subtle scent of fermentation; I liken it to the aroma of cut wood or grain. This acidic fragrance becomes stronger as the dough proofs, but it should never be vinegary. It's also generally more potent during summer, as the warmer climate helps foster a more robustly scented fermentation.

## SIGHT

I remember a day early on in my apprenticeship when Felix noticed that the dough was rising faster than normal. By sight alone, he could tell that we had forgotten to include the salt. After a taste to confirm, the batch went back into the mixer and the salt was added. In time, your eyes will know before the clock or timer that your dough has risen enough and is ready to be baked.

## SOUND

Your sense of sound is most engaged once the bread is out of the oven. Rapping on the loaf and listening to the sound is a good way to test if it's fully baked.

## TASTE

Taste is probably the most frustrating sense to rely on because it's hard to judge anything until after it's baked, and by then it's too late to fix! That said, a small taste of raw dough before baking can help you ascertain if you've forgotten an ingredient, and—especially in the beginning—it's also a very useful way to develop a sense of your preferred level of fermentation.

# Black Pepper Pain de Mie

Pain de mie, which Americans call a Pullman loaf, has a tender crumb and a slightly sweet flavor from the addition of milk. Because it is baked in a special lidded loaf pan, there's little expansion and no crowning, so the loaf slices into almost perfect squares. (Don't worry if you don't have the pan; you can use a regular loaf pan and foil.)

We add black pepper to our pain de mie, which creates a subtle floral flavor. It also helps make the perfect sandwich bread: already-seasoned slices that require only the filling. I like the pepper blend made by Olivier Roellinger of Épices Roellinger in Paris. Instead of a single flavor, his Poivre des Mondes (Peppers from the World) offers a concerto of notes. Or, you can make the pain de mie without the black pepper. The dough may rise slightly faster. The bread works well for savory applications, but I really love it spread with chocolate for an unusual sweet bite.

MAKES ONE 11-BY-4-INCH (28-BY-10-CM) PULLMAN LOAF OR ONE 9-BY-5-INCH (23-BY-13-CM) LOAF

294 g (2 cups plus 2 tablespoons) bread flour

98 g (¾ cup) all-purpose flour, plus more for dusting

1 tablespoon (13 g) sugar

1¾ teaspoons (5 g) active dry yeast

1¼ teaspoons (8 g) fine sea salt

2 teaspoons (5 g) Poivre des Mondes blend by Épices Roellinger (see Sources, page 277) or freshly ground black pepper

1 cup (240 ml) lukewarm (100°F to 110°F; 37°C to 43°C) whole milk

3 scant tablespoons (45g) lukewarm (100°F to 110°F; 37°C to 43°C) water

3 tablespoons (1½ ounces; 42 g) unsalted butter, softened

Neutral oil, such as canola, for the pan

In the bowl of a stand mixer fitted with the hook attachment, combine both flours, the sugar, and yeast. Mix in the salt and pepper. With the mixer on low, gradually add the milk and water and knead until a dough forms, about 1 minute. Add the butter 1 tablespoon at a time, waiting until it's almost completely blended before adding the next, and continue mixing until all the butter is incorporated and the dough is elastic and sticky, about 3 minutes.

Turn the dough out into an oiled bowl, cover with plastic wrap or a damp kitchen towel, and set aside in a warm (72°F to 77°F/22°C to 25°C), draft-free place until almost doubled in size, 2 to 2½ hours.

Oil an 11-by-4-inch (28-by-10-cm) Pullman loaf pan or a 9-by-5-inch (23-by-13-cm) loaf pan. Lightly flour a work surface.

continued

Turn the dough out onto the work surface and knead it gently to press out any large bubbles; be careful not to deflate the dough too much. Gently stretch two opposite sides of the dough and fold them over into the center. Stretch and fold the top and bottom of the dough over to form a ball. Gently shape the dough into a log about the length of the pan.

Transfer the dough to the pan seam side down, tucking the ends underneath if necessary to create a smooth, even top. Oil enough plastic wrap to cover the dough and cover the pan with it, oil side down. Let rest in a warm, draft-free place until the dough has risen to just about ½ inch (1.25 cm) from the top of the pan, 30 minutes to 1½ hours, depending on the temperature where it is rising (begin checking early).

Meanwhile, about 25 minutes before baking, position a rack in the lower third and preheat the oven to 400°F (200°C).

Remove the plastic wrap from the dough and, if using a Pullman pan, oil the lid and slide it on. Or, wrap the loaf pan tightly in a double layer of aluminum foil, oiling the part of the foil that will be in contact with the dough. (Be sure the ends of the pan are well wrapped too, or some dough might escape during baking.) Bake for 35 minutes.

Carefully remove the lid or foil, return the bread to the oven, and bake until the top is light brown, 10 to 15 minutes more; the center of the loaf should register between 190°F (88°C) and 210°F (99°C) on an instant-read thermometer.

Let the loaf cool in the pan for 15 minutes. Remove from the pan, transfer to a wire rack, and let cool completely before slicing. Stored in a plastic bag or wrapped in linen at room temperature, the pain de mie will keep for 2 to 3 days.

# Breakfast

# Breakfast

## So Important I Have It Twice

I'M ONE OF THOSE PEOPLE WHO NEEDS TO EAT SOON AFTER WAKING. Because my mother was American, I was raised eating breakfast fare like hot and cold cereal and toast, while most of my friends ate croissants or bread and butter. Over time, I have elaborated on the simple rolled oats and Cream of Wheat she used to cook, adding bold flavors like miso.

When I get up at four in the morning to visit our *Manufacture*, I pack a fruit smoothie or some granola to sustain me during the half-hour drive to it. I'm especially fond of my granola, which I developed using crumbs of our sourdough bread instead of the usual oats; it's lighter and has a toasty crunch.

Meanwhile, in the Cherche-Midi bakery, our customers breakfast on croissants, pains au chocolat, or bread, all of which disappear quickly during the morning hours. Patrons with heartier appetites grab a table in our café next door and enjoy a smoked salmon tartine or treat themselves to eggs en cocotte, our take on the classic egg-in-a-hole made with brioche toast.

On the mornings when I go directly from the *Manufacture* to the shop, I have a second breakfast around 8 a.m., when my retail team calls me down from my office to join them for breakfast. After the initial rush of customers, we gather in a small room separated from the shop by a frosted glass partition to eat, share stories, and gear up for the day ahead. Breakfast is informal and intimate, four or five of us total. We sit on old straw chairs around a table made from a retired bread-kneading box. On just about every part of the walls surrounding us hang the still lifes featuring our bread that artists painted for my grandfather in exchange for bread. Above us hangs a bread chandelier, each curved arm wrapped in baked dough, a whimsical fixture inspired by a collaboration between Salvador Dalí and my father.

We feast on fresh-baked breads and pastries, slathering our toast with soft cultured butter or jam. We're a diverse group from different parts of France and abroad, with strong identities, especially in regard to our food preferences. The Bretons like their butter salted, for example, and joke that because unsalted butter is such a rarity in those parts, one needs a prescription to get it there. Staff from northern France enjoy cheese in the morning, which is not something most Parisians do. Despite our differences, we all cherish breaking bread together and relaxing, even if just for a short period, while sharing stories about ourselves, including our own baking successes and recent favorite food finds. During Ramadan, a Moroccan staff member brings in pastries she's made. I've contributed a coconut jam I discovered on a visit to Southeast Asia. Slathered on our pain de mie, not only was it delicious, but it also bridged cultures. Along with the personal treats, we also sample any new breads, pastries, or cookies that the bakehouse is testing to offer feedback. Since I have usually already eaten a first breakfast, I'm not always hungry, but I crave the exchange of ideas that comes with this daily ritual.

What follows are some breakfast favorites, from the simplest toast (yes, there's a recipe!) to more involved but so-worth-it treats like brioche and croissants.

# OUR DALÍ BREAD

At Poilâne, art and bread are linked, forming a union of the bakery's neighborhood, my family's artistic tendencies, and the inherent symbolism within a loaf of bread. All of our bakeries feature paintings of our bread by local artists, which hang above the shelves holding our breads. Most date back to my grandfather's day, when artists in Saint-Germain-des-Prés occasionally paid for daily bread with a sample of their work. The paintings on the walls represent just a smattering of the hundreds we've collected over the years.

Most of the paintings in the back room at Cherche-Midi are of our sourdough, but the styles vary widely, from a dark, moody Vermeer-like scene of a sliced loaf and a brown clay pitcher to an abstract round on a bright red background to a black-and-white pencil sketch.

My father continued to celebrate the connection between bread and art through his friendships with artists, most significantly the Spanish surrealist Salvador Dalí, a regular visitor to the bakery. By the time my father met Dalí in the late 1960s, the artist had long been incorporating bread themes into his artworks. Dalí said, "Bread has been one of the oldest subjects of fetishism and obsession in my work, the first and the one to which I have remained the most faithful." Throughout their friendship, my father and Dalí engaged in endless conversations regarding the meaning of bread in life and art. So when Dalí decided to use dough as a medium, he naturally turned to my father, commissioning him to help create a bedroom suite made out of bread. (The notion allegedly stemmed from Dalí wanting to learn if there were mice in his room at the five-star hotel Le Meurice, where the installation was eventually displayed.) Our chandelier in the back room of our office in the Cherche-Midi shop is a replica of the one my father made for Dalí. We have to remake the chandelier every couple of years, because although bread may be a symbol of life, like life, it doesn't last forever, a paradox that was not lost on Dalí.

In another collaboration, this time for a performance piece, my father constructed a birdcage from bread. The live bird placed inside eventually ate its way through the bars of the cage. The work reminded my father of how he felt when working as a reluctant apprentice in his father's basement bakery. "I too felt like a bird in a cage made out of bread," he said. "I just fed on my limits."

To me, his birdcage embodies the nourishment my father managed to find in the profession he was compelled to enter.

# Perfect Toast

A recipe for toast? You may scoff, but my father was onto something with a little trick he had when it came to making toast. By putting two thin slices into one toaster slot at the same time, you get double the texture: the moistness of untoasted bread on one side and the crispness of toast on the other. You hear the sound that good toast makes when bitten into but with a lovely supple bite. This method also allows you to make a big batch ahead of time, because the toast doesn't dry out as fast, making it practical for a large group.

MAKES 2 SLICES

Two ½-inch (1.25-cm)-thick slices Poilâne-Style Sourdough (page 50), preferably about the same size

Softened butter, preferably salted cultured (see page 76)

Pair up the pieces of bread and place them in a single toaster slot. Toast to your liking; I like mine golden. *(The unbuttered toast can be held, covered with a linen cloth, for up to 15 minutes.)* Butter the toasted sides and serve.

# Homemade Cultured Butter

In France and other parts of Europe, butter is cultured by adding live bacteria to the cream before churning. The cream sits at room temperature long enough to ferment (culture). The result is butter with a slight tang and nuttiness. You can buy cultured butter, but it's easy (not to mention fun) to make it at home. (Bonus: After you "churn" the cream, there will be some residual liquid—i.e., buttermilk.)

Because there are so few ingredients, buy the best you can. For the cream, look for one with a high percentage of fat and try to avoid ultra-pasteurized, which tends to have less flavor. For the yogurt, be sure it has active cultures and, for best flavor and texture, avoid those with added stabilizers; the ingredient list should contain only milk and yogurt cultures.

**MAKES ABOUT 8 OUNCES (227 G) BUTTER AND 1 CUP (240 ML) BUTTERMILK**

2 cups (480 ml) heavy cream, preferably not ultra-pasteurized

2 tablespoons (30 ml) plain yogurt (any style; be sure the label specifies "live active cultures")

Ice water

¼ teaspoon (1.5 g) fine sea salt (optional)

In a medium bowl, whisk together the heavy cream and yogurt until combined. Cover with cheesecloth or perforated plastic wrap. Let stand at room temperature until the mixture has thickened slightly and gives off a slightly sour and tangy aroma, at least 18 hours, and up to 24 hours. Then refrigerate for 1 hour, or until chilled.

Transfer the cream mixture to a food processor and process until the curds begin to separate from the buttermilk, 3 to 4 minutes; the mixture will look like liquidy cottage cheese.

Line a fine-mesh sieve with cheesecloth and set it over a bowl. Strain the curd mixture through the cheesecloth. Gather the edges of the cheesecloth up around the solids and squeeze to force out as much of the liquid as possible. Remove the solids from the cheesecloth and place in a medium bowl. Refrigerate the liquid, which is buttermilk, for another use.

Pour ½ cup (120 ml) ice water over the solids and, using a rubber spatula, "wash" the butter by folding it over itself and pressing down to extract any remaining buttermilk. Drain off the milky liquid and discard it. Repeat the process, adding more ice water, until the liquid remains clear, which may take 4 or 5 rinses. The butter will start to harden, and it may become easier to work with your hands.

Lightly pat the butter dry with paper towels. If using salt, knead it in. Pack the butter into a bowl or jar and cover tightly, or roll it into a log and wrap in wax or parchment paper. The butter will keep in the refrigerator for about 3 weeks or in the freezer for several months.

# Flavored Jams

At the bakery, we sell jams made by the acclaimed Alsatian pastry chef Christine Ferber (see Sources, page 277), so we often have one of her distinctive jars with its polka-dotted red fabric "hat" on our breakfast table. Some of her jams, such as vanilla-rhubarb, are flavored. Although I don't often make jam from scratch, Christine's inspired me to add flavorings to some of my favorite preserves.

The following suggestions are all for a single serving, because once the jams are combined with fresh ingredients they don't keep well.

### RASPBERRY-APPLE

Add 1 tablespoon (7 g) chopped apple to 2 tablespoons (32 g) raspberry jam.

### BLUEBERRY-ORANGE BLOSSOM

Add 2 or 3 drops orange blossom water and a few sliced almonds to 2 tablespoons (32 g) blueberry jam.

### STRAWBERRY-MINT

Add 1 large pinch chopped fresh mint to 2 tablespoons (32 g) strawberry jam.

### BLACKBERRY-HAZELNUT

Add 1 teaspoon (3 g) chopped toasted and skinned hazelnuts to 2 tablespoons (32 g) blackberry jam.

### MEDITERRANEAN MARMALADE

Add a pinch ground cumin and a drop or two of rose water to 2 tablespoons (32 g) orange marmalade.

# Croissants

Though the croissant—made from a yeasted dough folded around a slab of butter and rolled to create layers of buttery, flaky goodness—probably hailed from Austria, it was perfected in France, where it has rightfully become iconic. Some pastry chefs like a brioche-esque, almost cakey croissant, but I'm partial to one with a drier, flakier texture because I prefer the way that a flaky croissant reveals its layers as you nibble it.

Some people begin by biting off both tips, which tend to be the crispest pieces. Others work their way from one end to the other. Here's my method: First I break off one tip, then I gently pull up the top of the exposed edge, unraveling the layers like yarn off a skein and eating it in bits as I go. That way, each bite alternates between crisp exterior and soft interior.

Because this recipe makes more than a dozen croissants, I have included ideas for using them, such as for sandwiches (page 162) and in a bread pudding (page 220). You can also split the dough into two portions and use half for plain croissants and half for pains au chocolat (page 86). Making croissants isn't hard, but it does take time. You can spread the work over a few days or even weeks. You can also freeze the unbaked croissants, which means you can have warm homemade croissants ready for lucky family or friends at breakfast.

NOTE: Since croissants rely on butter for flavor, buy the best you can afford, preferably a European cultured butter (see page 76), which has a high fat content and a deep flavor.

MAKES 14 CROISSANTS

370 g (2¾ cups) all-purpose flour, plus more for dusting

125 g (¾ cup plus 2 tablespoons) bread flour

¼ cup (55 g) sugar

1 package (2¼ teaspoons; 7 g) active dry yeast

1 cup (240 ml) lukewarm water

¼ cup (60 ml) whole milk, at room temperature

2 teaspoons (12 g) fine sea salt

2½ sticks (10 ounces; 284 g) unsalted butter, preferably cultured (see Note), softened

1 large egg, beaten with 1 tablespoon (15 ml) water for egg wash

In the bowl of a stand mixer fitted with the paddle attachment, combine both flours, the sugar, and yeast. In a separate bowl, vigorously whisk the water, milk, and salt until the salt dissolves. Add the mixture to the flour and mix on medium-low speed just until the dough comes together.

Switch to the dough hook (or, if you're kneading by hand, transfer to a lightly floured work surface). Increase the speed to medium-high and knead until the dough is smooth and somewhat elastic, about 5 minutes. Transfer the dough to a clean

continued

bowl, cover with a towel or plastic wrap, and refrigerate for at least 6 hours, and up to overnight.

Meanwhile, in a stand mixer fitted with the paddle attachment and in a clean bowl, beat the butter on medium speed until smooth. Scrape the butter onto a piece of parchment paper or plastic wrap, shape it into a 6-inch (15-cm) square, and store in a cool area. (You want the butter just malleable and not cold; you can refrigerate it, but let it soften at room temperature before using it.)

Lightly flour a work surface. Transfer the dough to the surface and roll it into a 9-inch (23-cm) square. Position the butter block on the dough square so that each corner of the butter square points at the middle of one side of the dough. Gently pulling on one corner of the dough, lift and stretch the flap over the butter block until it just reaches the center of the block. Repeat with the other corners of the dough to completely envelop the butter, then pinch the seams together to seal in the butter.

Turn the dough over and roll it out into a 20-by-10-inch (50-by-25-cm) rectangle. With a long side of the rectangle facing you, fold one third of the left side of the dough over the center, then fold the dough from the right side over that, so the dough is folded like a business letter. Use a dry pastry brush to brush off excess flour (too much flour will cause the croissants to be tough). Wrap the dough in plastic wrap and refrigerate for at least 45 minutes, and up to 2 hours.

Remove the dough from the refrigerator and roll it out toward the open sides into another 20-by-

10 inch (50-by-25-cm) rectangle. Fold again as described in the previous step; this is your first turn. Chill for another 2 hours. Repeat the rolling, folding, and chilling process two more times, for a total of 3 turns.

After the final turn, wrap the dough in plastic wrap and refrigerate for at least 1 hour. (*At this point, the dough can be refrigerated overnight or frozen for up to 3 months; defrost overnight in the refrigerator before shaping and baking.*)

When you're ready to form the croissants, line two baking sheets with parchment paper.

Unwrap the chilled dough. Cut it in half and wrap one half in plastic wrap and refrigerate while you work with the other half. (Or, if you like, use the other half to make a half batch of pains au chocolat, page 86; or freeze the other half for up to 3 months.)

Roll the half you are working with into a 20-by-10-inch (50-by-25-cm) rectangle. (If the dough resists rolling at any point, wrap in plastic wrap and refrigerate for 10 minutes to let it relax.) Using a knife or pizza cutter, cut the dough into 7 isosceles triangles (equal on two sides), each with a base of about 4½ inches (11.5 cm). You'll end up with little scraps of dough at each end; if you like, roll these into smaller, less perfectly shaped croissants as a baker's treat.

continued

Make a ½-inch (1.25-cm) vertical cut in the middle of each triangle's base; this makes it easier to roll the triangles up. Gently pull on the tip of one triangle to stretch it slightly, and then, starting at the base and splaying it out slightly where it's cut, roll the triangle up toward the point. Set the croissant on the baking sheet with its point tucked underneath so it doesn't unroll while rising. Curl in the tips and pinch the tips closed; they will spread open during proofing, but this helps the croissant keep its curved shape. (I like my croissants well rounded, with the ends curled in like the legs of a crab. This is not only aesthetically pleasing, attesting to extra attention to detail on the part of the baker, but it also reflects the pastry's original inspiration, the crescent moon.)

Repeat with the remaining triangles, being sure to leave at least 1½ inches (3.75 cm) between them to allow them to rise without touching. Then repeat the same cutting and shaping with the remaining dough if making the full batch. (*At this point, the shaped croissants can be chilled overnight, but they will take longer to rise in the next step. They can also be frozen for up to 3 months. Place them, still on the baking sheets, in the freezer until firm, then store airtight in a freezer bag for up to 3 months. Before baking, defrost overnight in the refrigerator, then let rise at room temperature on a parchment-lined baking sheet.*) Cover the croissants with a kitchen towel or plastic wrap and let rise in a warm, draft-free place until nearly doubled in size, about 2 hours. (If your home is cool—under 75°F/24°C—place a tray of just-boiled water in the bottom of your oven and, without turning it on, place the croissants in the oven to rise. Make sure you remove them before you preheat the oven for baking.)

Position a rack in the upper and lower thirds and preheat the oven to 425°F (220°C).

Using a pastry brush, gently brush the croissants with the egg wash. Bake until they are a deep golden brown, about 15 minutes, rotating the pans from top to bottom and front to back halfway through. Serve the croissants warm or at room temperature. Store any leftovers in an airtight container for up to 2 days.

# CROISSANT CONNECTIONS

Our croissants link the end of the nighttime baking shift and the start of a new day at the bakery. Their buttery scent as they're brought up from the basement to the storefront heralds the opening of the shop. Just as they bridge the night and morning worlds, they connect the worlds of the bread baker and the pastry chef.

In the baking world, croissants are categorized as *viennoiseries* (Viennese pastries), a category of yeasted doughs enriched with butter and sugar. But because, like bread, they contain yeast, they're often found at the boulangerie as well as the pâtisserie.

Deeply associated with French culture, the croissant is enveloped in flaky layers of lore. It's supposedly a descendent of the Austrian *kipfel*, a crescent-shaped cookie that, the story goes, was baked to celebrate the Ottomans' retreat from Vienna in 1683. (The cookie's curved shape resembles the moon on the Ottoman flag.) The cookie was brought to Paris by an Austrian baker named August Zang in the nineteenth century and evolved into the pastry we know today. For me, the crescent moon–shaped croissant symbolizes the time most bakers are hard at work, when the moon is the brightest light in the sky, even when it's just a sliver—or, as we say in French, a *croissant de lune*.

# Pains au Chocolat

Let me make something clear: Pain au chocolat is not, as some say, a "chocolate croissant." I'm sorry if I sound stern, but this is something I feel strongly about! While made from the same dough, the pain au chocolat is folded differently. The shape, plus the block of chocolate baked within, results in a pastry unique in both form and flavor.

Though I don't have a big sweet tooth, I do love chocolate. Our pains au chocolat have always been made with the highest-quality chocolate, but I always wished it wouldn't harden as the pastries cooled. This desire led me to partner with the esteemed chocolate maker Michel Cluizel to create a bar specifically for our pains au chocolat. The wide bars (which offer a proper mouthful) remain supple long after baking. You can find bars made by Cluizel in the U.S. (see Sources, page 277). Or choose another excellent eating chocolate.

**MAKES 12 PAINS AU CHOCOLAT**

| | |
|---|---|
| 370 g (2¾ cups) all-purpose flour, plus more for dusting | 2 teaspoons (12 g) fine sea salt |
| 125 g (¾ cup plus 2 tablespoons) bread flour | 2½ sticks (10 ounces; 284 g) unsalted butter, preferably cultured (see page 76), softened |
| ¼ cup (55 g) sugar | 12 pieces semisweet chocolate, each about 3 inches (7.6 cm) long, 1 inch (2.5 cm) wide, and ¼ inch (0.6 cm) thick |
| 1 package (2¼ teaspoons; 7 g) active dry yeast | |
| 1 cup (240 ml) lukewarm water | 1 large egg, beaten with 1 tablespoon (15 ml) water for egg wash |
| ¼ cup (60 ml) whole milk, at room temperature | |

In the bowl of a stand mixer fitted with the paddle attachment, combine both flours, the sugar, and yeast. In a separate bowl, vigorously whisk the water, milk, and salt until the salt dissolves. Add the mixture to the flour and mix on medium-low speed just until the dough comes together.

Switch to the dough hook (or, if you're kneading by hand, transfer to a lightly floured work surface). Increase the speed to medium-high and knead until the dough is smooth and somewhat elastic, about 5 minutes. Transfer the dough to a clean bowl, cover with a towel or plastic wrap, and refrigerate for at least 6 hours, and up to overnight.

Meanwhile, in a stand mixer fitted with the paddle attachment and in a clean bowl, beat the butter on medium speed until smooth. Scrape the butter onto a piece of parchment paper or plastic wrap, shape it into a 6-inch (15-cm) square, and store in a cool area. (You want the butter just malleable and not cold; you can refrigerate it, but let soften at room temperature before using.)

Lightly flour a work surface. Transfer the dough to the surface and roll it into a 9-inch (23-cm) square.

continued

Position the butter block on the dough square so that each corner of the butter square points at the middle of one side of the dough. Gently pulling on one corner of the dough, lift and stretch the flap over the butter block until it just reaches the center of the block. Repeat with the other corners of the dough to completely envelop the butter, then pinch the seams together to seal in the butter.

Turn the dough over and roll it out into a 20-by-10-inch (50-by-25-cm) rectangle. With a long side of the rectangle facing you, fold one third of the left side of the dough over the center, then fold the dough from the right side over that, so the dough is folded like a business letter. Use a dry pastry brush to brush off excess flour (too much flour will cause the pastries to be tough). Wrap the dough in plastic wrap and refrigerate for at least 45 minutes, and up to 2 hours.

Remove the dough from the refrigerator and roll it out toward the open sides into another 20-by-10-inch (50-by-25-cm) rectangle. Fold again as described in the previous step; this is your first turn. Chill for another 2 hours. Repeat the rolling, folding, and chilling process two more times, for a total of 3 turns.

After the final turn, wrap the dough in plastic wrap and refrigerate for at least 1 hour. (*At this point, the dough can be refrigerated overnight or frozen for up to 3 months; defrost overnight in the refrigerator before shaping and baking.*)

Line two baking sheets with parchment paper.

Unwrap the chilled dough. Cut it in half and wrap one half in plastic wrap and refrigerate while you work with the other half. Roll the half you are working with into a 20-by-10-inch (50-by-25-cm) rectangle. If the dough resists rolling at any point, wrap in plastic wrap and refrigerate for 10 minutes to let it relax.

Cut one rectangle of dough into six 3½-by-10-inch (8.5-by-25 cm) strips.

With a short end of one strip facing you, place a piece of chocolate about 2½ inches (6.35 cm) from the top of it, parallel to the top edge.

Roll and fold the dough over the chocolate, ending with the seam underneath (this is important; otherwise the rising pastries can tip over and unfold). Transfer to the baking sheet and repeat with the remaining strips and chocolate, leaving about 1 inch (2.5 cm) space between them to allow them to rise without touching. Roll out the remaining dough into a 20-by-10-inch (50-by-25-cm) rectangle as before, cut into 6 strips, and roll and fold the dough over the chocolate as directed. You will have a total of 12 pains au chocolat. (*The assembled pastries can be refrigerated overnight, but they will take longer to rise in the next step. They can also be frozen for up to 3 months: Place them, still on the baking sheets, in the freezer until firm, then store airtight in a freezer bag. Before baking, defrost on a parchment-lined baking sheet; they'll start rising once they've returned to room temperature.*)

Cover the shaped pains au chocolat with a piece of parchment paper and then a kitchen towel and let rise in a warm, draft-free place until nearly doubled in size, about 2 hours. (If your home is cool—under 75°F/24°C—place a tray of just-boiled water in the bottom of your oven and, without turning it on, place the pains au chocolate in the oven to rise. Make sure you remove them before you preheat the oven for baking.)

Position a rack in the upper and lower thirds and preheat the oven to 425°F (220°C).

Using a pastry brush, gently brush the tops of the pains au chocolat with the egg wash. Put the pains au chocolat in the oven, immediately reduce the temperature to 375°F (190°C), and bake until golden brown, 20 to 22 minutes, rotating the baking sheets from top to bottom and front to back halfway through the baking time.

Serve the pains au chocolat warm or at room temperature. Store any leftovers in an airtight container for up to 2 days.

# Brioche

Although brioche can be enjoyed at any time of day, it is a classic French morning treat. Enriched with butter and eggs, it's light and airy, with a soft, tender crumb and a paper-thin crust. A thick slice of brioche, toasted until golden to bring out the buttery notes and give it a slight crunch, is one of life's great pleasures.

The bread can be a little tricky to make because the volume of eggs and butter make the dough soft and slippery. My father used to have me mix it by hand—arduous work—to get a real feel for the dough. (I'll go easier on you and suggest that you use a stand mixer to do the job.)

The charming domed top of the brioche forms as the dough rises high above its pan, but it can sometimes collapse. I've made plenty of homely batches myself, so I know that butter, jam, and other toppings go a long way in covering up misshapen loaves. You can also make delicious *pain perdu* (French toast; pages 97 and 144) from less-than-perfect slices.

MAKES TWO 9-BY-5-INCH (23-BY-13-CM) LOAVES

1 package
(2¼ teaspoons; 7 g)
active dry yeast

2 tablespoons (30 ml)
lukewarm water

500 g (3⅔ cups)
all-purpose flour,
plus more for dusting

¼ cup (55 g) sugar

1¼ teaspoons (7.5 g) fine
sea salt

5 large eggs, at room
temperature

2¼ sticks (9 ounces;
250 g) unsalted butter,
softened just until
pliable, plus more for the
bowls and pans

1 large egg, beaten with
1 tablespoon (15 ml)
water for egg wash

In a small bowl, combine the yeast and water. Set aside for 5 to 10 minutes, until the yeast has dissolved and the liquid is frothy.

In the bowl of a stand mixer fitted with the paddle attachment, combine the flour, sugar, and salt on low speed. Turn the mixer to medium-low speed and add the yeast mixture, then add the 5 eggs and beat until well combined.

Switch to the dough hook and, with the mixer still on medium-low, add the butter a little at a time, waiting until each addition is almost completely incorporated before adding the next (you can gradually increase the mixing speed as you add more butter); it will take 10 to 12 minutes to incorporate all of it. Then continue kneading until the dough pulls away from the sides of the bowl to form a ball around the dough hook and

continued

is very elastic, 5 to 10 minutes. The trick is not to overwork the butter to the point where it melts; on warm days, reduce the kneading time. (The dough will be slightly less well kneaded in that case, which is all right.)

Butter two large bowls. Divide the dough in half, shape into 2 balls, and transfer them to the bowls. Cover each bowl with plastic wrap or a kitchen towel and set aside in a warm (72°F to 77°F/22°C to 25°C), draft-free place until about doubled in size, 2 to 3 hours. (*At this point, the dough can be wrapped well and refrigerated for up to 2 days or frozen for up to 3 months.*)

Generously butter two 9-by-5-inch (23-by-13-cm) loaf pans. Gently remove one ball of dough from the bowl and, being careful not to tear or deflate the dough too much, gently stretch two opposite sides and fold them in to the center. Stretch and fold the top and bottom over to form a round shape. Gently form into a 9-inch (23-cm)-long log and nestle, seam side down, in one of the prepared pans. Repeat with the remaining ball of dough.

Cover loosely with plastic wrap and set aside in a warm, draft-free place until the dough rises to the top of the pans and looks as if it's about to overflow, 1½ to 2½ hours. (If the brioche does not look as if it's about to overflow after 2½ hours, proceed with the baking. Although a dome is lovely, you don't want to overproof the dough, or the loaf may be dense.)

Position a rack in the lower third and preheat the oven to 350°F (180°C).

Using a pastry brush, brush the tops of the loaves with the egg wash. Using a pair of scissors, snip each loaf 5 or 6 times down its length. Let rest for 5 minutes.

Bake the loaves until golden, 28 to 35 minutes. Immediately remove the loaves from the pans and cool completely on a wire rack before serving.

Wrapped in a linen cloth in a plastic bag at room temperature, the brioche will keep for 3 to 5 days.

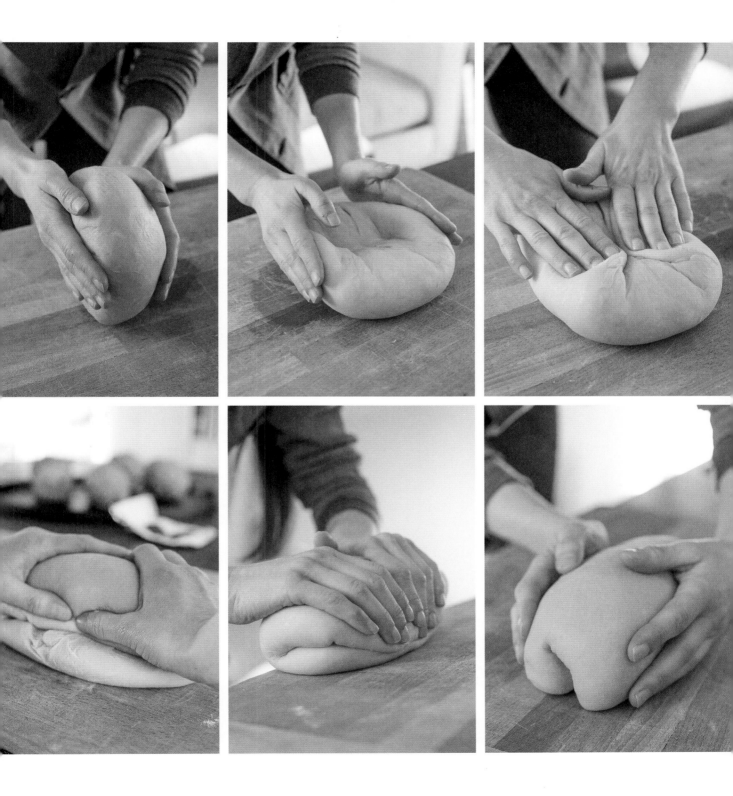

# Cardamom-Ginger–Swirled Brioche Feuilletée

*Feuilletée* may not be easy for non-French speakers to pronounce (try "foy-ay-tay"), but it's very easy to eat. It's made by rolling soft, buttery brioche dough around a spiced sugar filling to create amazing layers of flavor. I chose ginger and cardamom because the warm, tingly spices pair so well with coffee. (Funnily enough, I first came upon this morning pastry in Asia.) For the spices, I turned to Olivier Roellinger of Épices Roellinger, who crafted a blend called Poudre Kawa. However, you can come close to this mix by combining ground ginger and cardamom, as in the recipe.

MAKES ONE 9-BY-5-INCH (23-BY-13-CM) LOAF

**FOR THE SWIRL**

3 tablespoons (40 g) sugar

1½ tablespoons (9 g) Poudre Kawa (see Sources, page 277) or 1 tablespoon (6 g) ground ginger plus 1½ teaspoons (3 g) ground cardamom

**FOR THE FEUILLETÉE**

Softened butter, for the pan

1 ball Brioche dough (page 91), made through the first rise in the bowl

1 large egg, beaten with 1 tablespoon (15 ml) water for egg wash

**MAKE THE SWIRL:** In a small bowl, combine the sugar, ginger, and cardamom.

**MAKE THE FEUILLETÉE:** Generously butter a 9-by-5-inch (23-by-13-cm) loaf pan.

Roll the dough into a 14-by-8-inch (35.5-by-20-cm) rectangle. Sprinkle the swirl mixture evenly over the dough and then, starting from one of the shorter ends, roll it into a log. Cut it crosswise into thirds and place the 3 pieces swirl side up in the pan. Cover loosely with plastic wrap and set aside to rise in a warm (72°F to 77°F/22°C to 25°C), draft-free place until the dough reaches the top of the pan, 1½ to 2½ hours.

Position a rack in the lower third and preheat the oven to 350°F (180°C).

Using a pastry brush, brush the loaf with the egg wash. Let rest for 5 minutes. Bake the loaf until golden, 28 to 35 minutes. Immediately remove the loaf from the pan and cool completely on a wire rack before slicing.

Stored in a plastic or linen bag at room temperature, the brioche will keep for 3 days.

---

**NOTE:** If you would like to make 2 loaves, use both balls of brioche dough and double the amount of the swirl mixture.

# Eggs en Cocotte

This dish is one of the most popular breakfast items at our London café. Our take on the classic British dish egg-in-a-hole is made with a slice of brioche that has a hole cut out of it. The bread gets a swipe of mustard to offset its sweetness, an egg is cracked into it, and it's fried in a skillet. Then the whole thing is blanketed with cheese and broiled till melty. In effect, the bread acts as a casserole dish (*cocotte*); hence our name for it.

SERVES 2

Two 1½-inch (3.75-cm)-thick slices Brioche (page 91) or other brioche

2 teaspoons (1 g) chopped tender herbs of your choice, plus more for garnish (optional)

1 tablespoon (½ ounce; 14 g) unsalted butter, softened

1 teaspoon (5 g) whole-grain mustard

2 large eggs

Fine sea salt and freshly ground black pepper

2 ounces (57 g) mild or sharp cheddar, thinly sliced

Preheat the broiler to low.

Using a 2-inch (5 cm) round cutter (or a knife), cut a hole out of the center of each brioche slice; reserve the cutouts.

Toast the cut-out pieces under the broiler. Coarsely grind them and mix with the fresh herbs, if using.

Set a large ovenproof nonstick skillet over medium heat. Brush one side of each bread slice with some of the butter, place in the skillet, and cook until golden on the bottom. Remove from the heat, flip, and brush the untoasted sides with the remaining butter. Flip again so the browned side is up.

Spread the mustard on the top of the slices. Crack an egg into each hole and season with salt and pepper. Cover the pan and cook until the egg whites are set, 1½ to 2 minutes.

Uncover the pan, top the toasts with the cheese, and place the pan under the broiler until the cheese is bubbling. Transfer to plates, sprinkle with the brioche crumbs, and serve immediately, sprinkled with some more herbs, if you like.

# Pain Perdu with Roasted Rhubarb and Strawberries

The term *pain perdu* (French toast) means "lost bread" and is so named because it uses bread that might otherwise go to waste. Here golden, fried slices of brioche are topped with berries and rhubarb flavored with vanilla and cardamom.

SERVES 4 TO 6

**FOR THE RHUBARB AND STRAWBERRIES**

1 pound (450 g) rhubarb, trimmed and cut on the bias into ½-inch (1.25-cm)-thick slices (about 3¼ cups)

1 pint (340 g) strawberries, hulled and halved or quartered, depending on size

½ cup (110 g) sugar

Grated zest and juice of 1 lime

1 vanilla bean, split, seeds scraped out

½ teaspoon (1 g) ground cardamom

**FOR THE PAIN PERDU**

1 cup (240 ml) whole milk

2 large eggs, lightly beaten

½ cup (60 g) confectioners' sugar, sifted, plus more to finish

Fine sea salt

6 tablespoons (3 ounces; 85 g) unsalted butter

Six 1-inch (2.5-cm)-thick slices Brioche (page 91) or other brioche

**MAKE THE RHUBARB AND STRAWBERRIES:**
Toss all the ingredients except the cardamom together in a 9-by-13-inch (23-by-33-cm) baking dish. Let sit at room temperature until the rhubarb begins to release its juices and the sugar starts to dissolve, at least 20 minutes, and up to 2 hours.

Preheat the oven to 350°F (180°C).

Roast the rhubarb and strawberries, tossing once about halfway through, until tender but not falling apart, 20 to 25 minutes. Let cool completely.

Using a slotted spoon, transfer the rhubarb and strawberries to a bowl. Pour the remaining juices into a liquid measuring cup with a pour spout and stir in the cardamom.

**MAKE THE PAIN PERDU:** Position a rack in the middle and preheat the oven to 150°F (65°C), or to warm.

In a large shallow bowl, whisk the milk, eggs, confectioners' sugar, and a pinch of sea salt until the sugar dissolves.

Melt 2 tablespoons of the butter in a large skillet over medium-high heat. Working in batches, dip the brioche slices in the egg mixture, turning so they're thoroughly coated, and transfer to the pan. Cook, flipping once, until golden brown on both sides, about 6 minutes total, melting more butter between batches. Transfer to a plate and place in the oven to keep warm while you cook the remaining brioche.

Transfer the pain perdu to plates and serve, topped with the rhubarb and strawberries, the reserved liquid, and confectioners' sugar.

# Bread Granola

I love the versatility of granola and enjoy it as a stand-alone snack, with milk and yogurt, or even sprinkled over ice cream. In this version, chunks of dry bread take the place of the usual oats. This is a terrific way to use up leftover bread, especially breads with nuts or dried fruit. For more crunch and flavor, I add puffed rice and finely chopped hazelnuts and almonds. The result is crispy, crunchy, chewy, and just slightly sweet. Feel free to tweak the recipe using your favorite breads and different puffed grains and nuts. You can even add chopped dried fruit.

SERVES 6 TO 8

1 pound (450 g) Walnut Sourdough (page 52) or other sourdough, 2 to 3 days old, cut into 1-inch (2.5-cm) chunks (about 10 cups)

½ cup (57 g) whole hazelnuts, toasted and cooled

½ cup (57 g) whole almonds, toasted and cooled

½ cup (9.3 g) puffed rice

¾ cup (177 ml) wildflower honey

Fine sea salt

Position a rack in the middle and preheat the oven to 325°F (170°C).

In a food processor, process the bread to coarse crumbs. Transfer to a large bowl and set aside. Add the hazelnuts and almonds to the food processor and process until coarsely chopped. Add them to the bowl with the bread crumbs.

Add the puffed rice and toss to combine. Add the honey and a pinch of salt and toss to coat. Transfer the granola to a large baking sheet and bake, stirring every 10 minutes, until golden and fragrant, 35 to 40 minutes. Let cool completely.

Stored at room temperature in an airtight container, the granola will keep for up to 3 months.

# My Favorite Cereal Bowls

Cereal bowls are a relatively new addition to French breakfasts. But growing up with an American mother, I kicked off my days with crossovers between hearty Anglo-Saxon dishes and lighter French fare. The first two recipes below are cold cereals made with a combination of grains, nuts, and flavorings. Hearty and healthy, they are easy to prepare and can be made ahead.

The third recipe is for a warm cereal. On cold winter mornings, my mother would make us Cream of Wheat from boxes brought back from her trips to the United States. She always topped each bowl with a teaspoon of honey, but as I grew up, I began to experiment with other toppings—sweet and savory—according to the evolution of my taste and my mood. Here I add miso butter, for a combination I first had in New York City. The salty, creamy butter melting into the warm porridge provides the right balance to start my day.

## COLD PISTACHIO-ROSE OAT-BARLEY BOWL

Combine 1 cup (90 g) old-fashioned rolled oats, 1 cup (100 g) rolled barley flakes, 3 tablespoons (20 g) coarsely ground pistachios, the leaves from 4 dried organic rosebuds, and ¼ teaspoon (large pinch) ground fennel seeds. The cereal can be stored in a cool, dry place for up to 3 months.

You'll need to plan ahead when you want to have a bowl in the morning: The night before, for each serving, combine ⅓ cup (30 g) of the cereal with 1 cup (240 ml) milk (dairy or an alternative milk such as oat or almond) and refrigerate overnight. Serve cold.

## RYE-FLAX CEREAL WITH HAZELNUTS AND BEE POLLEN

Combine 1½ cups (150 g) rye flakes, ¼ cup (45 g) flax seeds, ¼ cup (25 g) chopped hazelnuts, and 2 tablespoons (25 g) bee pollen (see Sources, page 277). The cereal can be stored in a cool, dry place for up to 3 months.

The night before, for each serving, combine ⅓ cup (41 g) of the cereal with 1 cup (240 ml) milk (dairy or an alternative milk such as oat or almond) and refrigerate overnight. Serve cold.

## CREAM OF WHEAT WITH MISO BUTTER

Combine 2 tablespoons (1 ounce; 28 g) unsalted butter with 1 tablespoon (18 g) miso, preferably barley miso. Prepare the Cream of Wheat according to the package directions, and dollop in some of the miso butter just before serving.

# Oatmeal Smoothie

I first tasted a version of this oat smoothie in Japan. Made with blended oats and thickened and sweetened with banana, it's delicious as is, but you can also tailor it to your liking by adding a tablespoon of raw cocoa powder, a pinch of grated lime zest, or some honey.

You can buy ready-made oat milk, but you can easily make it at home. If you use homemade, shake it before you measure it.

MAKES 2 CUPS/480 ML; SERVES 2

1 ripe banana

1 cup (240 ml) oat milk, homemade (page 261) or store-bought

¼ cup (22.5 g) old-fashioned rolled oats

Crushed ice

In a blender, combine the banana, oat milk, and oats. Add crushed ice and blend until smooth. Pour into two glasses and serve immediately.

# INTELLIGENT HANDS, INTELLIGENT SPACE: THE MANUFACTURE

ON MANY WEEKDAY MORNINGS, WELL BEFORE THE SUN RISES, I DRIVE TO THE TOWN OF BIÈVRES, about ten miles southwest of Paris, to visit one of my favorite places in the world: our *Manufacture*. Within this low-slung white stucco building surrounded by fields and forest, Poilâne bakers work around the clock making more than 5,000 loaves of bread every day, plus pastries, all by hand, exactly as is done at Cherche-Midi.

I've been coming here all my life. My mother was pregnant with me at its grand opening in 1983, so I feel a special kinship to the building, which reflects a blend of both my parents' professions. Believing hands are more intelligent than a machine, my father devised an expansion plan that was both retro (the bread would all be made by hand) and innovative; he called his methodology *retro-innovation*. In response, my mother designed a unique miche-shaped building to make that dream a reality. Together, they chose a location that feels the opposite of industrial, a rural hilltop with grasses, flowers, and trees as far as the eye can see.

If my window is down as I pull into the driveway, I can smell the sweet fragrance of the white flowers of the *sarcococca*, evergreen shrubs that bloom even in the winter, which we planted along the driveway to help awaken the senses of our early-morning drivers. The building is aglow with light, which I can see through the large windows that line its perimeter. Through the windows, I see loaves of sourdough cooling on racks. More important, the bakers can see out to the natural world that surrounds them. The inclusion of an expansive view was very important to my father, who despised being confined to the windowless basement bakery at Cherche-Midi.

The bright white foyer does not resemble a lobby of a production facility so much as it does an art gallery. And indeed, as with all of our bakeries, there is art on display here. To my left as I enter is a sculpture by the Italian artist David Reimondo, whose medium is literally sliced bread, which he toasts and then fashions into maps, landscapes, or, in this case, a life-size human form. Paintings of our bread similar to those on display at Cherche-Midi hang on the walls, along with framed photos of my family.

At this early hour, all of the orders are local. Later, after the next shift of bakers finishes up their work, FedEx trucks will whisk boxes of bread to their nearby international hub at Charles de Gaulle airport. From there, those loaves, packed while still warm, will be flown to more than forty different

continued

countries so that bread lovers around the world can enjoy our bread with dinner the next day.

As I make my way down the curved white hallway that forms the outer ring of the circular building, the large windows stream light into the twelve baking rooms (*fournils*) positioned like spokes off the corridor. These bright, airy rooms are fashioned after the setup of the basement bakehouse at Cherche-Midi. The baking rooms include two of everything: two mixers, two proofing boxes, two shaping tables, two ovens—replicas of my grandfather's original—and two bakers.

The design is a direct result of the fact that my father hated working alone when he apprenticed for my grandfather. Each baker makes up to 300 loaves per shift, managing his own oven as if he were in a stand-alone bakery, but he can enjoy the company of a colleague while doing so. This doubling-up also helps newly trained bakers, because they can work with a master baker alongside. With these rooms, on any given shift, we can have up to twenty-four bakers making bread at the same time.

Keeping twenty-four brick ovens going requires a lot of wood, so the entire center of the building contains massive piles that practically touch the domed twenty-foot-high ceiling. These are clean scraps from the lumber industry that would otherwise go to waste. When my sister and I were kids, we would clamber up and down the stacks for fun. Nearby sits a car-size sculpture of a loaf of sourdough by Thierry Vidé, representing the amount of bread the average person eats in a lifetime.

My mother designed the building as a round to promote the easy movement of our product and people, and because that shape is found in nature. The *Manufacture* fits beautifully into the bucolic setting, with its abundance of wildflowers, old oaks, and acres of wheat and rye planted for our loaves.

Her forward-thinking design, with its malleable space, has allowed for expansion and evolution. In the years since my parents built the *Manufacture*, our business has grown so much that I had to expand the loading docks to make room for packing more goods.

I leave the *Manufacture* a little before 6:30 a.m. to get to Cherche-Midi by the time it opens. Soon after that, a new shift of bakers will clock in and work through the day. As I pull out of the driveway, it's still dark. Once again, I inhale the scents coming from the flowers; the aroma lingers while I make my way back to Paris just as the sun comes up over the Seine.

The forest outside the *Manufacture*.

# Afternoon

# THE MAIN MEAL, THE ART of KEEPING BREAD, and SWEETS

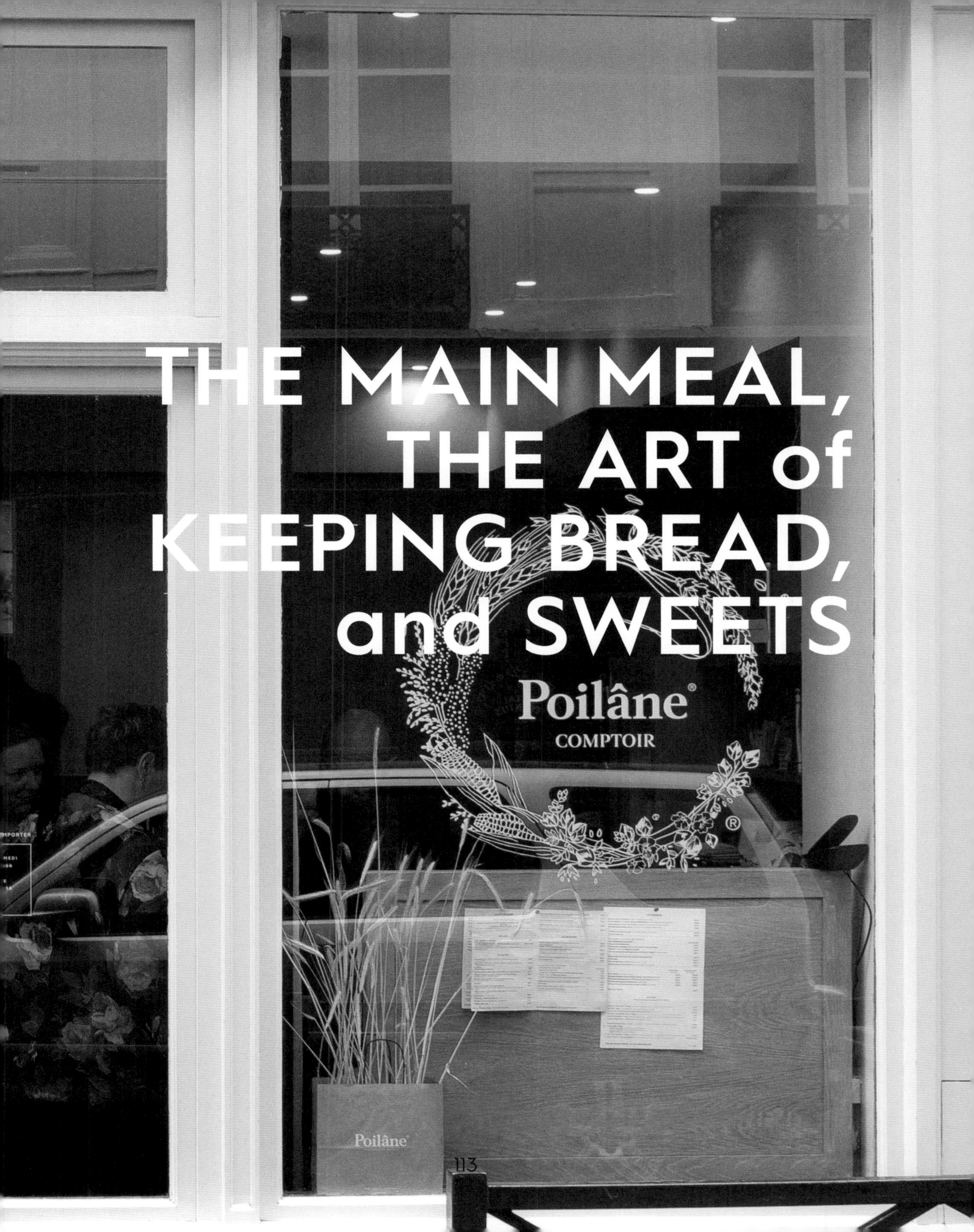

# The Main Meal

## Grain Salads

BLACK RICE AND QUINOA SALAD
WITH AVOCADO, PEAS, AND
YUZU KOSHO DRESSING 148
WHEAT AND RYE BERRY SALAD WITH
FENNEL, BEETS, AND TAHINI 152
GREEN TOMATO–FARRO SALAD 155
BARLEY AND CABBAGE SALAD WITH
STIR-FRIED BEEF 156
TRIPLE-CORN, CURRY, AND
CRAB SALAD 159

## Baked Camembert
Casse-Croûte 160

## Croissant Sandwiches 162

SMOKED SALMON AND CHIVE 162
HAM AND CHEESE 162
SAUTÉED GREENS AND COMTÉ
(OR GRUYÈRE) 162

## Walnut Bread–Parsley Pesto 165

## Winter Vegetable Crumble with
Citrus Bread Crumbs 166

## Meatloaf with Fresh Mint
and Peas 169

## Bread Crumb–Crusted Lamb with
Vegetables en Croûte 170

## Sweet Potato and
Sunchoke Stuffing 172

WHEN I WORK AT THE CHERCHE-MIDI BAKEHOUSE, I USUALLY STOP AT NOON AND HEAD HOME FOR LUNCH. I choose a still-warm loaf to bring with me, tucking it into my jacket, a great way to keep toasty on a wintry walk. At home, before I even start cooking, I cut a thick slice of bread and spread it with salted butter as a little treat to tide me over.

More often than not, bread not only accompanies my meal but also becomes a crucial component of it. I call this "breadcooking." If I pull together a salad, it's topped with freshly made croutons. If I'm having soup, it's often been thickened with sourdough bread. If I'm hosting friends for lunch, I coat pieces of fish in flavored bread crumbs and panfry them, or I hollow out a round of bread and bake some cheese in it for a fondue of sorts.

In France, lunch is not a grab-and-go affair. Traditionally it was the longer, more filling meal of the day, often comprising a few courses: a starter, such as cooked asparagus or a soup; a main course of fish or meat; a cheese course; and something sweet to finish. Now, especially during the workweek, the menu is shorter and lighter, but we still revere our midday meal.

When my sister and I were growing up, we went to a school nearby so we could come home for lunch. Despite their hectic work schedules, my parents almost always hosted a formal midday dinner, inviting guests from various sectors of their lives. On weekdays, Athena and I had only about an hour, so after saying hello to the guests, we ate in the kitchen, listening to the grown-ups discuss art, work, and life in the dining room. The assembled—young and old, artists and businesspeople, good friends and more casual acquaintances, many of them famous in the world of art, business, or politics—brought diverse interests and backgrounds to the table. These gatherings were what would today be called business lunches.

On Saturdays, my sister and I would join the adults in the dining room, and we were always expected to take part in the discussion. These lunches were as much a part of our education as school, and they were food for the body as well as the mind. I still believe sitting with people for the midday meal, something I strive to do most days, provides the necessary nutritional and intellectual fuel to get through the rest of the day.

My father's belief in the importance of lunch led him to open a café in 1996 right next door to our Cherche-Midi bakery. Called Bar de Cuisine, it was a casual place, with neither a fully equipped kitchen nor a highly trained chef. The simple menu featured our wheat sourdough as the base for a variety of classic tartines (open-faced sandwiches). As they waited, customers

could enjoy a green salad, which reflected an idiosyncrasy of my parents' own lunches at home, which invariably began with a salad. (In the typical French meal of that time, the salad followed the main course.)

Recently, I revamped and reopened the café, renaming it Comptoir Poilâne. *Comptoir* means "counter," and the word calls to mind the zinc counters in French cafés that bring people together as my parents did. I also intended the name to suggest *les comptoirs de commerce*, cities and trading posts that act as ports for culinary and cultural crossovers.

Our tartines are assembled in a tiny kitchen, the equipment consisting mostly of toaster ovens. The menu, which now includes breakfast, features a range of the breads baked daily, as well as salads and bowls featuring wheat and rye berries, farro, quinoa, and barley.

To me, Comptoir Poilâne feels like an extension of my home. The space is serene yet casual, and it caters to both personal and business occasions in the spirit of my parents' lunches.

The recipes in this chapter are inspired by the meals I grew up with at home, variations on my father's tartines, and items we prepare each day at Comptoir Poilâne. There are quick-to-make but satisfying dishes as well as more involved recipes that are easy to make ahead.

From my father's collections of paintings at our Comptoir Poilâne

# Zucchini and Black Garlic Gazpacho

Lunch at Comptoir Poilâne usually begins with soup or a green salad. This refreshing gazpacho is one of my favorite summertime starters. Most people think of gazpacho as tomato-based, but before tomatoes came to Europe from the New World, there was *ajo blanco*, a Spanish precursor made from bread, almonds, garlic, and olive oil. My recipe is close to that soup in spirit, and the baker in me loves that it transforms bread into something drinkable.

Black garlic, made by aging garlic until it's dark and rather sticky, is sweet and earthy but without the hot sharpness of regular garlic. If you only have the latter, use half the amount, as noted below. As for the black licorice powder, it underscores the subtle licorice-like flavor of black garlic. If you don't have it, use some black pepper instead.

Although the soup is quick to make, the bread and zucchini need to macerate in the oil and vinegar for at least 6 hours, so plan ahead.

SERVES 4 TO 6

8 ounces (230 g) day-old Poilâne-Style Sourdough (page 50) or other sourdough, or Black Pepper Pain de Mie (page 64) or other sandwich bread, crusts removed, cut into ¾-inch (2-cm) pieces (about 4 cups)

1 medium zucchini, peeled and coarsely chopped

4 black garlic cloves (see headnote and Sources, page 277) or 2 regular garlic cloves, finely chopped

⅓ cup (80 ml) extra-virgin olive oil

¼ cup (60 ml) rice wine vinegar

About 2 cups (480 ml) cold water

Fine sea salt

Licorice root powder (see headnote and Sources, page 277) or freshly ground black pepper

In a medium bowl, combine the bread, zucchini, garlic, olive oil, and vinegar and toss well. Cover with plastic wrap and refrigerate for at least 6 hours, and up to 24 hours.

Transfer the mixture to a blender. Add ½ cup (120 ml) of the cold water and blend, adding more water about ½ cup (120 ml) at a time, until you have the consistency you want. Season to taste with salt and licorice powder or pepper.

Serve the soup right away, or cover and refrigerate for up to 2 days. If the gazpacho is very cold, taste and add more salt or licorice powder or pepper.

# Watermelon Panzanella

Panzanella, a salad of ripe, juicy tomatoes and croutons, was created as a way to use up day-old bread. Including watermelon in the mix brings a modern fresh flavor to this classic dish.

SERVES 4 TO 6

**FOR THE CROUTONS**

8 ounces (225 g) day-old Poilâne-Style Sourdough (page 50) or other sourdough, crusts removed, cut into 1-inch (2.5-cm) pieces (about 4 cups)

2 tablespoons (30 ml) extra-virgin olive oil

**FOR THE VINAIGRETTE**

¼ cup (60 ml) extra-virgin olive oil

3 tablespoons (45 ml) balsamic vinegar

Fine sea salt and freshly ground black pepper

8 ounces (225 g) watermelon flesh, cut into 1-inch (2.5-cm) pieces (about 3 cups), juices reserved

3 medium tomatoes, diced, or 1 pint cherry tomatoes, halved, juices reserved

8 ounces (225 g) cherry tomatoes, halved (about 1½ cups)

¼ cup (7 g) chopped fresh mint

**MAKE THE CROUTONS:** Preheat the oven to 400°F (200°C).

On a large baking sheet, toss the bread cubes with the olive oil. Bake, stirring once or twice, until the outsides of the cubes are crisp but the centers are still chewy, 8 to 10 minutes. Set aside to cool.

**MEANWHILE, MAKE THE VINAIGRETTE:** In a large bowl, whisk together the oil and vinegar. Season to taste with salt and pepper.

Add the watermelon and tomatoes and their juices to the vinaigrette and toss to coat. Add the croutons and toss. Set aside for at least 30 minutes, and up to 2 hours, before serving. Add the mint and serve.

# Caesar Salad with Brioche Croutons

This recipe solves two common problems with classic Caesar salad. The first is that although the croutons add texture, they're often bland. The second is that many people think they don't like anchovies. To "disguise" them and boost the croutons' flavor, I season the bread cubes with anchovies pureed with garlic, lemon zest, and mustard. Once toasted, the croutons burst with a rich, savory taste that even non-anchovy lovers enjoy.

I like brioche for croutons because it offers a slightly softer crunch. The salad on its own makes a fine lunch, but you can add grilled shrimp or chicken.

Note that the bread needs to soak in the anchovy puree for at least 6 hours.

**SERVES 6**

8 ounces (225 g) Brioche (page 91) or other brioche, cut into 2½-inch (6.5-cm)-thick slices

12 oil-packed anchovies

1 garlic clove, chopped

Finely grated lemon zest from 1 large lemon

1 teaspoon (5 g) Dijon mustard

6 tablespoons (90 ml) water

Freshly ground black pepper

½ cup plus 1 tablespoon (135 ml) extra-virgin olive oil

3 tablespoons (20 g) freshly grated Parmigiano-Reggiano, plus more for serving

3 tablespoons (45 ml) fresh lemon juice

1 teaspoon (5 ml) honey

Fine sea salt

3 romaine hearts, leaves separated and roughly torn

Place the bread in a shallow dish large enough to hold the slices in a single layer.

In a blender, combine the anchovies, garlic, lemon zest, mustard, and water and puree until smooth. Season to taste with pepper.

Pour half of the puree over the brioche, turn the slices over, and pour over the remaining puree. Cover the dish with plastic wrap and refrigerate for at least 6 hours, and up to 24 hours.

Preheat the broiler.

Tear the brioche into 1-inch (2.5-cm) pieces. Place the pieces on a baking sheet, drizzle with 3 tablespoons (45 ml) of the olive oil, and sprinkle with the cheese. Broil, tossing once or twice, until the bread is toasted and golden, about 3 minutes. Remove from the heat.

In a large serving bowl, whisk together the lemon juice, the remaining 6 tablespoons (90 ml) olive oil, and the honey. Season to taste with salt. Add the romaine and toss well.

Serve the salad topped with the croutons and sprinkled with additional cheese.

# Beet Salad with Roquefort and Dukkah Croutons

Beets and blue cheese are a classic combination, and for good reason: The earthy-sweet flavors of the vegetable pair perfectly with the tangy cheese.

Dukkah is an Egyptian spice-and-nut mixture that you can easily make yourself with readily available ingredients. Croutons coated in dukkah add both fragrance and crunch to this salad.

SERVES 6

¼ cup (60 ml) red wine vinegar

1 tablespoon (15 g) whole-grain mustard

1 tablespoon (15 ml) honey

1 garlic clove, grated or finely minced

Fine sea salt and freshly ground black pepper

6 tablespoons (90 ml) extra-virgin olive oil

4 medium peeled cooked yellow or candy cane beets, cut into ½-inch (1.25-cm) cubes

1 medium raw red beet, peeled and grated

⅔ cup (100 g) crumbled Roquefort

2 cups (120 g) Dukkah Croutons (page 186)

¼ cup (36 g) pistachios, toasted and chopped

In a medium bowl, whisk together the vinegar, mustard, honey, garlic, and a pinch each of salt and pepper. Whisking constantly, slowly add the olive oil, whisking until the dressing is emulsified and creamy.

Add the cooked and raw beets to the vinaigrette and toss to coat. Season to taste with salt. Divide the salad among six plates, top with the cheese, croutons, and pistachios, and serve.

# Roquefort, Bread Crumb, and Walnut Spread

The combination of rye and Roquefort is appropriate, since legend has it that the cheese came about after a shepherd in a cave left his loaf of rye bread near his maturing sheep's-milk cheese. Additionally, the sheep's-milk cheese rounds are known as *pains* ("loaves"). Serve this along with a crisp green salad for a starter or as part of an appetizer spread.

MAKES 2 CUPS

1⅔ cups (228 g) crumbled Roquefort cheese

8 tablespoons (4 ounces; 113 g) unsalted butter, softened

¼ cup (25 g) fine bread crumbs (see page 181), preferably from Rye Loaf with Currants (page 60)

¼ cup (30 g) walnuts, toasted and coarsely chopped

Dried fruit, such as apricots, dried cherries, and dried pears, for serving

Crackers, Bread Chips (page 182), and/or slices of Rye Loaf with Currants (page 60), for serving

In a food processor or a blender, puree half of the cheese with the butter until very smooth. Transfer to a large bowl and stir in the remaining cheese, the bread crumbs, and walnuts.

Spoon the mixture into a small dish or jar. Cover and refrigerate for at least 1 hour, and up to 3 days. Remove from the refrigerator about 45 minutes before serving.

Serve the spread with dried fruit and crackers, bread chips, and/or slices of bread.

# Bread Crumb Tabbouleh

Peek into a Parisian's picnic basket and you may just find tabbouleh, the bulgur salad featuring loads of chopped parsley and tomatoes, seasoned with olive oil, lemon juice, salt, and pepper. In France, we tend to make the dish with more grain than the classic version, which is all about the parsley. I make mine with toasted bread crumbs, which have a texture similar to bulgur. This tabbouleh retains the fresh, vibrant feel of the original, and the tang of the sourdough crumbs balances the sweetness of the ripe tomatoes.

SERVES 4 TO 6

2 tablespoons (30 ml) extra-virgin olive oil

2 cups (130 g) finely ground bread crumbs (see page 181), preferably from Poilâne-Style Sourdough (page 50)

4 ripe medium tomatoes, diced

1 medium white onion, finely diced (optional)

4 loosely packed cups (120 g) coarsely chopped fresh flat-leaf parsley

½ cup (15 g) coarsely chopped fresh mint

Juice of 2 lemons

Heat the olive oil in a large skillet over medium heat. Add the bread crumbs and cook, stirring occasionally, until golden and crisp, 5 to 8 minutes. Transfer to a large serving bowl and set aside to cool.

Add the tomatoes, onion, if using, parsley, mint, and lemon juice to the bowl and mix to combine. Cover the bowl with plastic wrap and refrigerate for at least 2 hours, and up to 6 hours, before serving.

Serve the tabbouleh chilled.

# Lionel Poilâne's Bread Sandwich

My father was a playful man, so when he first described his bread sandwich—
a piece of thin bread, buttered and toasted, sandwiched between two buttered
slices of untoasted bread—I thought he was joking. Beyond its deliciousness, my
father wanted to illustrate the idea that bread is a fully self-sufficient food, in no
need of a separate filling.

Originally he made his with three slices of our Poilâne-Style Sourdough
(page 50). I prefer our Rye Bread (page 59), either plain or currant-studded
(page 60), as the center slice. Either way, the contrast between the soft and crispy
bread and the salted and unsalted butter is memorable.

Make sure to use the best butter you can find—it makes all the difference.

MAKES 1 SANDWICH

Two ½-inch (1.5-cm)-
thick slices Poilâne-Style
Sourdough (page 50) or
other sourdough

1½ tablespoons (¾ ounce;
21 g) unsalted butter,
softened

One ¼-inch (0.6-cm)-
thick slice Rye Bread
(page 59), Rye Loaf with
Currants (page 60), or
other rye bread

1½ tablespoons
(¾ ounce; 21 g) salted
butter, preferably
cultured (see page 76),
softened

Use a butter knife or small spatula to lightly
spread one side of each slice of sourdough with
the unsalted butter.

Toast the slice of rye until crisp and golden and
lightly butter it on both sides with the salted butter.
Sandwich the toasted bread between the untoasted
slices, buttered sides in, and eat right away.

# Croque Mademoiselle

You've likely heard of croque monsieur, a grilled ham and cheese sandwich topped with béchamel sauce, and croque madame, the same sandwich with an egg on top. Croque mademoiselle is a lighter, more contemporary variation with a vegetable filling in lieu of—or in addition to—the traditional ham. I make mine with sautéed zucchini and caramelized onions flavored with a bit of mustard and thyme. Instead of a heavy béchamel, the bread gets a light coating of cheese. I like to serve it topped with an egg, but you can go with just the sandwich on its own.

MAKES 2 SANDWICHES

1½ tablespoons (22 ml) extra-virgin olive oil, or as needed

1 small onion, thinly sliced

Fine sea salt and freshly ground black pepper

½ medium zucchini or summer squash, trimmed and sliced lengthwise into ⅓-inch (0.8-cm)-thick slices

4 slices Black Pepper Pain de Mie (page 64) or other sandwich bread

2 teaspoons (5 g) whole-grain mustard

1½ teaspoons (1 g) finely chopped fresh thyme or 2 pinches dried thyme

4 thin slices good-quality cured ham, such as jambon de Bayonne or prosciutto (optional)

2 tablespoons (1 ounce; 28 g) unsalted butter, melted

2 tablespoons (18 g) freshly grated Parmigiano-Reggiano

2 fried eggs (optional)

In a large skillet, heat the oil over medium-high heat. Add the onion and cook, stirring occasionally, until very soft and caramelized, 20 to 25 minutes. Season with salt and pepper. With a slotted spoon, transfer the onion to a plate; do not wipe out the skillet.

Add the zucchini slices to the pan in a single layer (if there isn't enough oil left from the onion, add a little more) and cook until golden on the first side, 3 to 4 minutes. Flip and cook on the other side until golden and tender, 3 to 4 minutes more. Transfer the zucchini to the plate with the onion and set aside. Wipe out the skillet.

Spread one side of 2 slices of the bread with 1 teaspoon of the mustard each and sprinkle with the thyme. Divide the onion evenly between the bread slices and top with the zucchini slices and 2 slices each of ham, if using. Finish with the remaining bread slices.

Heat the skillet over medium-low heat. Brush one side of each sandwich with some of the melted butter and place the sandwiches butter side down in the skillet. Cook, adjusting the heat as necessary, until golden on the first side, about 1 minute. Brush the unbuttered side with the remaining melted butter, flip the sandwiches, and top each with a tablespoon of the cheese; it should melt in the time it takes to brown the second side, about 2 minutes.

Top each sandwich with a fried egg, if you like, and serve hot.

# Tartines

Tartines, a much prettier way of saying "open-faced sandwiches," have become very popular in the United States, and for good reason: They make a substantial lunch; they are a great way to use whatever ingredients you have on hand; and, because their ingredients are often layered and carefully arranged, they can look stunning on the plate. A tartine can be simple—smashed avocado and a drizzle of oil—or indulgent, such as the ham and cheese Tartine for Bon on page 136. And a tartine cut into small pieces becomes an easy spur-of-the-moment hors d'oeuvre.

Our sourdough makes the perfect base for these sandwiches. The slices are large with a tight crumb, and it toasts beautifully. My golden rule is never make a topping higher than what you can pick up with one hand (or than what you can eat neatly with a fork and knife).

As with buttered toast (see page 75), I prefer my tartine bread toasted on one side only. This way, you get that crisp texture, but because one side is still soft, the bread is easy to slice or bite. I also like a balance of flavors and a pop of color.

The recipes that follow are based on long slices of sourdough. Depending on the size of your bread, you may need to use two slices. You can also fiddle with the amounts of toppings.

# Tartine for Bon

This is our most popular tartine, and it has been on the menu since the original café opened in 1996. Perhaps that's why my father named it "Tartine for Good." Then again, he may have been alluding to the fact that the classic pairing of ham and cheese is always good. What makes this tartine a standout, though, is the type of ham and cheese we use. For the cheese, I prefer Saint-Marcellin, small rounds of mold-ripened cow's-milk cheese from Southwest France that's often sold in small terra-cotta dishes or wrapped in chestnut leaves. The cheese is creamy and Brie-like, with a thin, wrinkly rind, and its personality changes as it ripens, going from mild, with a soft texture, to complex, with a nutty, fruity mushroom flavor and runny texture. Bayonne ham, which is air-cured, could be considered France's prosciutto; use the latter if you can't find Bayonne.

**MAKES 2 TARTINES**

Two 1-inch (2.5-cm)-thick slices Poilâne-Style Sourdough (page 50) or other sourdough

2 tablespoons (1 ounce; 28 g) salted butter, preferably cultured (see page 76), softened

2 rounds (170 g) Saint Marcellin cheese or other soft and creamy cow's-milk cheese, such as Brie

6 thin slices (85 g) jambon de Bayonne or other cured ham, such as prosciutto

Freshly ground black pepper

Large pinch herbes de Provence (optional)

Preheat the broiler to low.

Spread the bread with the butter. Slice each round of cheese through the middle to get 2 rounds, then cut each round in half. If using Brie or another cheese, slice ⅓ inch thick. Lay the cheese across the slices of bread. Top with the ham and sprinkle with pepper. Broil until the ham is crisp, 2 to 3 minutes.

Sprinkle the herbes de Provence, if using, over the top and serve immediately.

# Fresh Goat Cheese and Salmon Roe Tartine

You can think of the combination of goat cheese and salmon roe as a French spin on cream cheese and lox. But instead of a bagel, it goes on a slice of our sourdough. I love the pop and flavor of salmon roe, and the glistening orbs look gorgeous, but you can substitute thinly sliced cured or smoked salmon, or use a combination of the two.

MAKES 2 TARTINES

Two 1-inch (2.5-cm)-thick slices Poilâne-Style Sourdough (page 50) or other sourdough

2 ounces (56 g) fresh goat cheese, crumbled (about ¼ cup), at room temperature

2 radishes, sliced paper-thin

1 tablespoon (14 g) salmon roe

½ teaspoon (2 pinches) finely grated lemon zest

Toast the sourdough on one side until golden.

Spread the goat cheese evenly over the toasted sides of the bread. Layer the radishes over the cheese and top with the salmon roe. Sprinkle with the lemon zest and serve.

# Avocado Tartine with Banana and Lime

This take on avocado toast is topped with banana slices. A drizzle of honey and a sprinkle of red pepper flakes add sweetness and heat, and a little lime juice balances the flavors. Also try it for breakfast or brunch.

**MAKES 2 TARTINES**

Two 1-inch (2.5-cm)-thick slices Poilâne-Style Sourdough (page 50) or other sourdough

1 ripe medium avocado, halved, pitted, peeled, 4 thin slices reserved, the rest coarsely mashed

1 medium banana, sliced

1 teaspoon (2 g) finely grated lime zest

2 tablespoons (30 ml) fresh lime juice

Crushed red pepper flakes

1 to 2 tablespoons (15 to 30 ml) honey

Toast the sourdough on one side until golden.

Spread the mashed avocado over the toasted sides of the bread. Arrange the banana and avocado slices on top. Sprinkle with the lime zest, drizzle with the lime juice, and finish with a pinch or two of the pepper flakes. Drizzle with the honey and serve.

# Apple, Comté (or Gruyère), and Caramel Tartine

This tartine straddles the line between lunch and dessert, and it also makes a great appetizer or snack. The tartness of the apple complements the rich cheese and the sugary caramel. You need only a couple of tablespoons of this sauce for the tartine, but it keeps well. A tiny bit of lemon juice helps prevent the sugar from crystallizing as it caramelizes but does not affect the flavor. If you prefer not to mix sweet and savory, replace the caramel with whole-grain mustard.

MAKES 2 TARTINES; 1 CUP CARAMEL

¾ cup (150 g) sugar

⅓ cup (80 ml) water

¼ teaspoon (1 ml) fresh lemon juice

⅓ cup (80 ml) heavy cream

6 tablespoons (3 ounces; 85 g) unsalted butter, cut into pieces

Two 1-inch (2.5-cm)-thick slices Poilâne-Style Sourdough (page 50) or other sourdough

1 Granny Smith apple, cut into matchsticks

8 very thin slices Comté or Gruyère cheese

Flaky sea salt

**MAKE THE CARAMEL SAUCE:** In a small heavy-bottomed saucepan, combine the sugar, water, and lemon juice, bring to a boil over medium-high heat, and cook, without stirring (swirl the pan occasionally for even cooking), until the sugar melts and the caramel is amber, 10 to 15 minutes. (Once the caramel begins to color, it will darken quickly, so watch carefully.)

Immediately remove the pan from the heat and add the cream; be careful, as the mixture will bubble and steam. Return the pan to medium-low heat and stir until smooth. Add the butter a few pieces at a time, stirring until melted. Cool the sauce slightly.

**MAKE THE TARTINES:** Toast the sourdough on one side until golden.

Spread the caramel evenly on the toasted sides of the bread. Place the apple and cheese slices over the caramel, sprinkle each tartine with a pinch of flaky salt, and serve with additional caramel sauce, if you like.

---

**NOTE:** To store the caramel, let cool to room temperature, cover, and refrigerate for up to 1 month. To reheat, microwave on high, stirring every 20 seconds, or heat in a small saucepan over medium-low heat, stirring. Feel free to add a pinch of salt if using the caramel for a different recipe.

# Savory Pain Perdu

In this savory version of French toast, the custard for the brioche is flavored with tomatoes and curry powder. It makes a fantastic lunch or brunch, especially when paired with a simple green salad.

SERVES 4 TO 6

6 very ripe medium tomatoes, coarsely chopped

1 teaspoon (2 g) curry powder, such as Madras

1 teaspoon (6 g) fine sea salt, plus more to taste

2 large eggs, lightly beaten

4 tablespoons (60 ml) extra-virgin olive oil, plus more as needed

4 fresh chives, finely chopped

Freshly ground black pepper

3 tablespoons (1½ ounces; 42 g) unsalted butter, plus more if needed

Six 1-inch (2.5-cm)-thick slices Brioche (page 91) or other brioche

Position a rack in the middle and preheat the oven to 150°F (65°C), or to warm.

In a blender, combine one-quarter of the chopped tomatoes, the curry powder, and salt and blend until pureed. Transfer to a large shallow bowl and whisk in the eggs.

In a medium bowl, toss the remaining tomatoes with 1 tablespoon (15 ml) of the olive oil and the chives. Season to taste with salt and pepper and set aside.

In a large skillet, heat 1 tablespoon (15 ml) of the olive oil and 1 tablespoon (14 g) of the butter over medium heat. Working in batches, dip the bread into the tomato-egg mixture, turning to thoroughly coat, then transfer to the pan. Cook, adjusting the heat as needed and flipping the bread once, until golden brown on both sides, about 6 minutes total. Transfer to a baking sheet and keep warm in the oven while you cook the remaining bread, adding more butter and oil to the pan as needed.

Serve the pain perdu warm, topped with the chopped tomatoes.

# Tenzin's Bread Maki

When we were exchanging memories about our childhood snacks, my friend Tenzin, who grew up in North America and Asia, told me that for an afternoon treat, he flattens a piece of bread, spreads peanut butter and jelly on it, rolls it up, and eats it like a sushi roll. He jokingly calls it maki. Inspired by his idea, I use nori and bread for these savory mayo-anchovy rolls. Ultra-fresh bread is best for this recipe.

**MAKES 12 PIECES**

2 thin slices Black Pepper Pain de Mie (page 64), Rye Bread (page 59), or other sandwich bread, crusts removed

2 sheets nori (untoasted)

2 tablespoons (28 g) mayonnaise

1 teaspoon (5 g) wasabi paste

1 tablespoon (9 g) toasted sesame seeds

4 oil-packed anchovies

½ medium cucumber, peeled, halved lengthwise, seeded, and cut into matchsticks

Using a rolling pin, flatten the bread slices to about ¼ inch (0.6 cm). Trim them so they're about the same size as the nori. Place the bread on top of the nori.

In a small bowl, stir together the mayonnaise and wasabi. Spread the mixture evenly over the bread squares. Sprinkle with the sesame seeds. Place 2 of the anchovies and half of the cucumber slices horizontally across the bottom third of one bread square, carefully roll up into a tight cylinder, and wrap in plastic. Repeat with the second bread square and the remaining ingredients. If not serving right away, wrap the rolls in a cloth (to absorb any moisture) and refrigerate.

To serve, remove the plastic, lightly moisten a sharp knife, then cut each into 2 to 4 pieces.

# Smoky Cauliflower Gratin

You can use any type of bread for this recipe; crumbs from rye bread will bring woody accents, while those from sourdough will bring more acidity. My favorite crumbs here are made from our Black Pepper Pain de Mie (page 64) because the pepper complements the cauliflower's creaminess.

SERVES 4 AS A MAIN COURSE, 6 AS A SIDE

½ cup (70 g) salted smoked almonds

½ cup (64 g) coarsely ground bread crumbs (see page 181)

½ cup (43 g) coarsely grated Parmigiano-Reggiano

Fine sea salt and freshly ground black pepper

1 large head cauliflower, cored and cut into small florets

3 tablespoons (45 ml) extra-virgin olive oil

Juice of 1 lemon

2 garlic cloves, grated or finely minced

½ teaspoon (1 g) sweet smoked paprika

Preheat the oven to 350°F (180°C).

In a food processor, pulse the almonds until they are ground to a fine powder. Add the bread crumbs and cheese and pulse just to combine. Season with salt and pepper.

Steam the cauliflower in a steamer basket in a large pot until just tender, 8 to 10 minutes.

Transfer the cauliflower to an 8-inch (20-cm) square baking dish. Add 2 tablespoons (30 ml) of the olive oil, the lemon juice, garlic, and paprika and toss to coat. Season to taste with salt and pepper. Sprinkle with the bread crumb mixture and drizzle with the remaining 1 tablespoon (15 ml) olive oil.

Bake until the bread crumbs are toasted, 15 to 20 minutes. Serve warm.

# Black Rice and Quinoa Salad with Avocado, Peas, and Yuzu Kosho Dressing

Yuzu kosho, a spicy paste made of yuzu (a Japanese citrus peel), garlic, chile, and salt, appeals to my love of all things fermented, but, more important, here it adds an aromatic acidity that balances the subtle sweetness of the black rice and punches up the flavors of this brilliant springtime salad. And the salad's varied textures, with creamy avocado, crunchy walnuts, and a mix of chewy quinoa and tender rice, make it hard to stop eating, as each bite brings a different adventure.

SERVES 6 TO 8

1 cup (200 g) black rice, rinsed well

4 cups (960 ml) water

Fine sea salt

1 cup (175 g) quinoa, rinsed well

3 tablespoons (45 ml) fresh lemon juice

1 tablespoon (15 ml) white wine vinegar

1 tablespoon (15 g) Dijon mustard

2 teaspoons (10 g) red yuzu kosho (or substitute more fresh lemon juice)

1 shallot, thinly sliced

1 garlic clove, finely chopped

⅔ cup (160 ml) extra-virgin olive oil

Freshly ground black pepper

4 cups (280 g) cooked peas or shoots, or other favorite shoots, such as alfalfa, sunflower, or broccoli

1 avocado, halved, pitted, peeled, and sliced

1 cup (100 g) walnuts, toasted and chopped

In a medium saucepan, combine the rice and 2 cups (475 ml) water, season with salt, and bring to a boil. Reduce the heat to low, cover, and cook until the rice is tender and the water is mostly absorbed, 35 to 40 minutes. Drain if necessary, fluff with a fork, and let cool.

Meanwhile, in another medium saucepan, combine the quinoa and the remaining 2 cups (475 ml) water, season with salt, and bring to a boil. Reduce the heat, cover, and cook until mostly tender with a delicate crunch, 15 minutes. Drain the quinoa and return it to the pot. Let the quinoa sit off the heat and covered for 5 minutes. Fluff with a fork and let cool.

Transfer the rice and quinoa to a large serving bowl. (*Both the rice and quinoa can be made ahead, covered, and kept at room temperature for up to 1 hour or refrigerated for a few hours. If they've been refrigerated, let sit at room temperature for up to an hour before serving.*)

continued

In a medium bowl, whisk together the lemon juice, vinegar, mustard, and yuzu kosho (or additional lemon juice). Stir in the shallot and garlic and set aside to macerate for 10 to 15 minutes.

Whisking constantly, slowly pour the olive oil into the yuzu kosho mixture and continue whisking until the dressing is emulsified and creamy. Season to taste with salt and pepper.

Just before serving, add the peas or pea shoots to the rice and quinoa and toss to combine. Drizzle with the vinaigrette and toss to coat. Season to taste with salt and pepper and toss again. Top with the avocado and walnuts and serve.

# Wheat and Rye Berry Salad with Fennel, Beets, and Tahini

With a mild flavor and nubby texture, this grain and vegetable salad spiked with cloves, orange, and maple is perfect for the colder months. Toasting the wheat and rye berries brings out their personalities. Serve as a main course or as a side for roast chicken or meats, or use it as a poultry stuffing.

SERVES 6 AS A MAIN COURSE, 10 AS A SIDE

¾ cup (130 g) rye berries, rinsed

¾ cup (130 g) wheat berries, rinsed

1 orange

⅓ cup (45 g) dried sour cherries or cranberries

¼ small red onion, thinly sliced

3 tablespoons (45 ml) red wine vinegar

⅛ teaspoon (0.3 g) ground cloves

Fine sea salt and freshly ground black pepper

¼ cup (60 ml) tahini

1 tablespoon (15 ml) maple syrup

⅓ cup (80 ml) extra-virgin olive oil

¼ cup (60 ml) ice water

1 fennel bulb, trimmed and thinly sliced

2 small beets, peeled and thinly sliced

Bring a large pot of well-salted water to a boil. Meanwhile, set a large skillet over medium heat, add the rye berries, and toast, stirring often, until slightly browned and fragrant. Transfer to a plate. Repeat with the wheat berries, placing them on a separate plate.

Add the rye berries to the boiling water, lower the heat to a rolling simmer, and cook until al dente, 1 hour to 1 hour 20 minutes. Use a sieve or slotted spoon to transfer the rye berries to a baking sheet or platter, spreading out the grains in an even layer. Cool completely.

Return the water to a boil, add the wheat berries, and cook until tender, about 35 minutes. Drain in a fine-mesh sieve and spread out on another baking sheet in an even layer to cool.

Meanwhile, finely zest half the orange. Cut the orange in half crosswise. Juice one half and reserve the juice. Use a paring knife to peel the skin off the other half. Free the orange segments by running the knife along the membranes. Coarsely chop the segments and reserve. In a medium bowl, combine the dried sour cherries or cranberries, onion, red wine vinegar, orange zest and juice, and cloves.

Season with salt and pepper. Set aside for at least 15 minutes, and up to 2 hours.

Drain the dried fruit in a fine-mesh sieve set over a large bowl; reserve the liquid. Transfer the cherry-onion mixture to a small bowl and set aside.

Whisk the tahini and maple syrup into the soaking liquid in the bowl. Whisking constantly, slowly pour in the olive oil and then the ice water and continue to whisk until the dressing is emulsified and creamy. Add the rye and wheat berries, fennel, beets, chopped orange, and the reserved cherry mixture. Toss to coat with the dressing and serve.

# Green Tomato–Farro Salad

Farro is a welcome addition to salads. It contains a lot of fiber and is deliciously chewy. (If you're not a patient cook, use the semi-pearled or pearled versions, which have had the thick bran removed.) Here I pair earthy farro with unripened green tomatoes. Along with fresh herbs and cumin, the tart tomatoes brighten this salad. If green tomatoes are unavailable, substitute regular tomatoes and add a bit of fresh lemon juice.

SERVES 6 TO 8

1 cup (190 g) farro (see headnote)

1½ tablespoons (21 ml) white wine vinegar

1½ teaspoons (7 g) Dijon mustard

Finely grated zest from 1 lemon

¼ teaspoon (1 large pinch/0.5 g) ground cumin, toasted briefly in a dry skillet over medium heat until fragrant

3 medium green (unripe) tomatoes, diced, juices reserved (see headnote)

½ cup (120 ml) extra-virgin olive oil

Fine sea salt and freshly ground black pepper

1 cup (50 g) coarsely chopped mixed fresh herbs (such as cilantro, mint, and parsley)

Bring a large pot of heavily salted water to a boil. Meanwhile, set a large skillet over medium heat, add the farro, and cook, stirring, until lightly toasted and fragrant, 1 to 2 minutes. Remove from the heat.

Add the toasted farro to the boiling water and boil until the farro is al dente, 20 to 25 minutes for pearled, longer for semi-pearled or whole. Drain in a fine-mesh sieve and transfer to a baking sheet or platter, spreading out the grains in an even layer. Cool completely.

In a small bowl, combine the vinegar, mustard, lemon zest, cumin, and the reserved tomato juices. Whisking constantly, slowly pour in the oil and continue whisking until the vinaigrette is emulsified and creamy. Season with salt and pepper.

Transfer the farro to a large serving bowl. Add the tomatoes and herbs and toss to combine. Drizzle with the vinaigrette, toss to coat, and season to taste with salt and pepper. Serve.

# Barley and Cabbage Salad with Stir-Fried Beef

Seasoned with ginger, scallions, garlic, and sesame oil, this salad can be served warm or cold. Beef's meaty flavor works well with the cabbage and hearty barley, but you could stir-fry chicken or shrimp in the same manner and top the salad with that. Though you can use regular soy sauce, dark soy sauce is richer and less salty.

SERVES 6

**FOR THE SALAD**

½ cup (100 g) pearled barley, rinsed

½ large savoy cabbage (about 900 g), cored, leaves thinly sliced (about 7 cups)

⅓ cup (80 ml) fresh lemon juice (from 2 lemons), or more to taste

¼ cup (60 ml) rice wine vinegar

1 tablespoon (15 ml) Asian sesame oil

1 teaspoon (5 ml) honey

One 1-inch (2.5-cm) piece fresh ginger, peeled and grated

1 garlic clove, grated or minced

½ cup (120 ml) extra-virgin olive oil

Freshly ground black pepper

2 large carrots, coarsely grated

2 scallions, thinly sliced

**FOR THE BEEF**

2 tablespoons (30 ml) soy sauce, preferably dark (see headnote)

2 teaspoons (10 ml) Asian sesame oil

2 teaspoons (5 g) cornstarch

1 to 1¼ pounds (500 to 575 g) lean beef, such as flank or sirloin, cut into ¼-inch (0.6-cm)-thick slices

Freshly ground black pepper

2 tablespoons (30 ml) neutral vegetable oil, such as canola

1 teaspoon (3 g) black sesame seeds

1 teaspoon (3 g) white sesame seeds

**MAKE THE SALAD:** Bring a large pot of well-salted water to a boil. Meanwhile, set a large skillet over medium heat, add the barley, and toast, tossing and stirring often, until slightly browned and fragrant. Remove from the heat.

Add the barley to the boiling water and boil until tender, 25 to 30 minutes. Drain in a fine-mesh sieve and transfer to a baking sheet or platter, spreading out the grains in an even layer. Cool completely.

Place the cabbage in a large bowl and sprinkle with 1 tablespoon (15 g) salt. Using your hands, massage the salt into the cabbage. Set aside for 15 minutes.

Fill the bowl of cabbage with cold water, stir the cabbage with your hands to rise off most of the salt, and transfer the cabbage to a colander to drain.

In a large bowl, whisk together the lemon juice, vinegar, sesame oil, and honey. Add the ginger and garlic. Whisking constantly, slowly pour in the olive oil and continue whisking until the vinaigrette is emulsified and creamy. Season to taste with salt, pepper, and, if desired, additional lemon juice.

Add the barley, cabbage, carrots, and scallions to the vinaigrette and toss to combine. Season to taste with salt and pepper. Set aside.

**MAKE THE BEEF:** In a large bowl, whisk together the soy sauce, sesame oil, and cornstarch. Season the beef with pepper, add it to the bowl, and toss to combine. Let marinate for 10 to 20 minutes.

In a large skillet, heat the oil over high heat. Add the beef and stir-fry until browned, about 3 minutes. Add the sesame seeds and toss to coat.

Serve the beef over the salad.

# Triple-Corn, Curry, and Crab Salad

A classic summer salad in France consists of canned corn, canned tuna, and chopped tomatoes. To be honest, I'm not a fan. However, I do think crab and corn pair well. My updated version, seasoned with curry powder, presents corn in three different ways: fresh, popped, and as cornflakes—but not canned. I like the light flavor and white color of the egg white omelet in this dish; if you want to make it with whole eggs, use three.

SERVES 4

2 medium carrots, grated

3 tablespoons (45 ml) fresh lemon juice

2 tablespoons (10 g) curry powder, such as Madras

3 tablespoons (36 g) popcorn kernels

¼ cup (60 ml) extra-virgin olive oil

4 large egg whites, lightly whisked (see headnote)

Fine sea salt and freshly ground black pepper

2 tablespoons (1 ounce; 28 g) salted butter

Fresh corn kernels from 2 ears corn (about 1½ cups)

Crushed red pepper flakes to taste (optional)

8 ounces (225 g) lump crabmeat, picked over for shells and cartilage

1 cup (30 g) unsweetened cornflakes

In a large serving bowl, toss together the carrots, lemon juice, and 1 tablespoon (5 g) of the curry powder.

Set a large pot over medium-high heat, add the popcorn kernels, 3 tablespoons (45 ml) of the olive oil, and the remaining 1 tablespoon (5 g) curry powder, cover, and cook, shaking the pot often, until all the kernels have popped.

Remove from the heat. Set a small nonstick skillet over low heat, add the remaining 1 tablespoon (15 ml) olive oil, and heat until warmed through. Add the egg whites, season with salt and pepper, and cook, without stirring, until the whites start to set. Using a rubber spatula, gently lift the eggs around the edges, letting the runny, uncooked egg whites flow underneath. When the omelet is completely set, transfer to a cutting board and let cool for 5 minutes. Using a knife, shred into bite-size pieces.

Increase the heat under the pan to medium-high and add the butter, corn kernels, and a large pinch of red pepper flakes, if using. Cook, stirring often, until the corn kernels are cooked through and beginning to brown, about 5 minutes.

Add the cooked corn, popcorn, shredded omelet, crab, and cornflakes to the carrot mixture, toss gently, and serve immediately.

# Baked Camembert Casse-Croûte

*Casse-croûte*, literally "the breaking of the crust," refers to a worker's lunch or a snack in which bread is the main ingredient. Typically a casse-croûte includes bread, cheese, and possibly ham. This dish is all about the bread and cheese. A hollowed-out walnut loaf is filled with cheese and baked until it's nice and melty. The reserved bread is toasted for dipping into the cheese.

The Camembert is a nod to my family's roots in Normandy—the birthplace of the fragrant cheese—and it also pairs well with the walnuts in the bread. Another round soft-rind cheese such as Brie (Brie Fermier is especially good), Jasper Hill Farm's Harbison, Old Chatham Camembert, or your own favorite can be substituted. This recipe can be prepared well ahead and makes an impressive appetizer. Don't toss the hollowed-out loaf when you're finished dipping into the cheese—it's the best part of the dish!

SERVES 4 TO 6

One 5- to 7-inch (13- to 17-cm) round Walnut Sourdough (page 52) or other nut loaf

One 3-inch (7.5-cm) round Camembert (see headnote)

1 tablespoon (15 ml) rosemary honey, or plain honey plus leaves from 1 large fresh rosemary sprig

Crudités for serving, such as carrots, bell pepper, and summer squash (optional)

Preheat the oven to 350°F (180°C). Line a baking sheet with aluminum foil.

Using a serrated bread knife, slice off the top third of the walnut loaf; reserve the top. Hollow out the center, reserving the bread you remove, to create a hole large enough to hold the Camembert. Slice the reserved bread into thin pieces (leave the top piece intact). Set aside.

Place the hollowed-out bread on the prepared baking sheet and place the Camembert in it. Slice an X in the top of the cheese. Trim so it fits. Spoon the honey over the top and sprinkle with the rosemary, if using. Replace the top of the bread. Wrap tightly in aluminum foil or parchment paper.

Bake until the cheese is melted and fragrant, about 40 minutes. Unwrap and serve hot with the reserved bread and with crudités, if desired, for dipping.

# Croissant Sandwiches

Growing up in Paris, I didn't encounter sandwiches made with croissants until my first semester of college in the States. It took a while to wrap my head around the idea of pairing a sweet pastry with savory fillings. However, as I spent time with friends trying out different combinations, I came to appreciate the idea. The best fillings include an acidic component to counter the buttery notes of the croissant. Here are some of my favorites.

EACH VARIATION MAKES 1 SANDWICH

## SMOKED SALMON AND CHIVE

Split a day-old croissant in half. Layer the bottom half with 2 slices smoked salmon, cucumber slices, and thin radish slices. Sprinkle with 1 teaspoon (5 ml) fresh lemon juice and ½ teaspoon (2 pinches) chopped fresh chives. Season with salt and pepper, top with the other half of the croissant, and serve.

## HAM AND CHEESE

Preheat the broiler.

Split a day-old croissant in half and place both halves cut side up on a baking sheet. Spread the bottom half with mustard to taste. Layer 2 slices good cured ham, such as jambon de Bayonne or prosciutto, and 2 slices white cheddar on the bottom half and season with pepper. Broil until the cheese melts and turns golden and fragrant, about 2 minutes. Top with the other half of the croissant and serve warm.

## SAUTÉED GREENS AND COMTÉ (OR GRUYÈRE)

Heat 2 tablespoons (30 ml) extra-virgin olive oil in a medium skillet over medium heat. Add 1 cup (28 g) thinly sliced greens, such as kale, collards, or spinach, and cook, stirring occasionally, until bright green and tender, about 3 minutes. Stir in 1 teaspoon (5 ml) white wine vinegar and season with salt and pepper. Remove from the heat.

Preheat the broiler.

Split a day-old croissant in half and place the greens on the bottom half. Top with sliced or grated Comté or Gruyère. Season with pepper and broil until the cheese melts and turns golden and fragrant, about 2 minutes. Top with the other half of the croissant and serve warm.

# Walnut Bread–Parsley Pesto

Walnut bread is a great replacement for both the nuts and the cheese in pesto. You can substitute a thick slice of Poilâne-Style Sourdough (page 50) and ¼ cup walnuts for the walnut bread here. Though basil is more traditional, I love the bold flavor of parsley, plus it's available year-round. Serve over pasta or on crostini.

MAKES 1¼ CUPS

2 thick slices Walnut Sourdough (page 52) or other walnut bread, diced (see headnote)

4 loosely packed cups (120 g) coarsely chopped fresh parsley (from 2 large bunches)

⅔ cup (160 ml) extra-virgin olive oil

Fine sea salt and freshly ground black pepper

In a food processor or blender, pulverize the bread into fine crumbs. Add the parsley and a few tablespoons of the olive oil and pulse until the parsley is coarsely chopped. Slowly pour in the remaining olive oil and process to a puree. Season with salt and pepper and pulse to combine. The pesto will keep, covered and refrigerated, for up to 5 days.

# Winter Vegetable Crumble with Citrus Bread Crumbs

Citrus-flecked bread crumbs lighten up this combination of parsnips, turnips, beets, and fennel. I especially like the crumble with bread crumbs made from our sourdough. The crumble will be prettier if you dice the vegetables, but you can just chop them if you're in a hurry. Serve as a vegetarian lunch or as a side dish.

SERVES 4 AS A MAIN COURSE, 6 AS A SIDE

½ cup (120 ml) extra-virgin olive oil

2 large onions, thinly sliced

Fine sea salt and freshly ground black pepper

4 garlic cloves, finely chopped

3 large carrots, peeled and sliced

2 large parsnips, peeled and sliced

1 fennel bulb, stalks removed, fronds reserved, and bulb diced into ½- to ¾-inch (1.5- to 2-cm) pieces

1 large or 2 small turnips, peeled and diced into ½- to ¾-inch (1.5- to 2-cm) pieces

2 medium yellow or red beets, peeled and cut into thin wedges

1 cup (128 g) coarsely ground bread crumbs (see page 181), preferably from Poilâne-Style Sourdough (page 50)

1 tablespoon (3 g) finely chopped reserved fennel fronds

⅓ cup (28 g) finely grated Parmigiano-Reggiano or other hard cheese (optional)

2 teaspoons (2 g) finely grated orange or grapefruit zest

Preheat the oven to 400°F (200°C).

Warm ¼ cup (60 ml) of the olive oil in a large skillet over medium-high heat. Add the onions, season with salt and pepper, and cook, stirring occasionally, until softened, about 5 minutes. Stir in the garlic and cook until softened, about 2 minutes. Transfer the mixture to a 9-inch (23-cm) square baking dish and spread it out evenly.

In a large bowl, toss the carrots, parsnips, fennel bulb, turnips, and beets with 2 tablespoons (30 ml) of the olive oil. Season well with salt and pepper. Spread over the onions in the baking dish.

Bake the crumble for 15 minutes, then reduce the heat to 350°F (180°C) and bake until the vegetables are just tender, about 45 minutes.

Meanwhile, in a medium bowl, combine the bread crumbs, chopped fennel fronds, the remaining 2 tablespoons (30 ml) olive oil, the cheese, if using, and the zest, and stir to mix.

Remove the baking dish from the oven and sprinkle with the bread crumbs. Bake until the crumbs are golden, about 15 minutes longer.

Serve warm or at room temperature.

# Meatloaf with Fresh Mint and Peas

This meatloaf was inspired by the classic British combination of lamb and mint. Here a combination of ground lamb and beef, seasoned with cumin and smoked paprika, is lightened by peas, mint, and bread crumbs.

SERVES 6 TO 8

¼ cup (60 ml) extra-virgin olive oil, plus more for drizzling

1 small sweet onion, such as Vidalia, finely chopped

1 leek, well washed, white and light green portions finely chopped

⅔ cup (44 g) finely ground bread crumbs (see page 181) from Black Pepper Pain de Mie (page 64) or other sandwich bread or Poilâne-Style Sourdough (page 50) or other sourdough

⅔ cup (160 ml) whole milk

1 pound (450 g) ground lamb

1 pound (450 g) ground beef (preferably 80% lean)

1 cup (140 g) fresh or thawed frozen peas

2 large eggs, lightly beaten

½ cup (15 g) finely chopped fresh mint

1½ teaspoons (10 g) fine sea salt

1½ teaspoons (3 g) ground cumin

½ teaspoon (1 g) smoked sweet paprika

Freshly ground Szechuan or black pepper (grind Szechuan in a spice grinder)

In a large skillet, heat the olive oil over medium-low heat. Add the onion and leek and cook, stirring occasionally, until very soft, 15 to 20 minutes. Remove from the heat and let cool completely.

Preheat the oven to 350°F (180°C). Oil a 9-by-5-inch (23-by-13-cm) loaf pan and set aside.

Meanwhile, in a large bowl, combine the bread crumbs with the milk. Set aside until the bread crumbs absorb the liquid.

Add the lamb, beef, peas, eggs, mint, salt, cumin, paprika, and a few grinds of pepper to the bread crumb mixture and mix gently with your hands to combine. Gently transfer the mixture to the prepared pan (don't pack it in) and drizzle with a little oil. *(You can refrigerate the meatloaf for a few hours before baking; cover well with plastic wrap, and remove it from the refrigerator while the oven heats up.)*

Bake until the meatloaf has released some juices and an instant-read thermometer inserted into the center registers 160°F (70°C), 50 minutes to 1 hour. Invert the meatloaf onto a cutting board, turn right side up, and let rest for 10 minutes before slicing and serving.

# Bread Crumb–Crusted Lamb with Vegetables en Croûte

This was the meal my parents made to impress: a boneless leg of lamb, fragrant with cumin and cardamom and coated in a crisp, golden bread crumb crust. The bread accompanying the roast is just as dramatic. The large hollowed-out loaf acts like an edible Dutch oven to cook the vegetables, maintaining an even temperature so they come out tender and fresh-tasting. You can certainly prepare either the lamb or the vegetables alone, but rather than throwing out the bread from the hollowed-out loaf, doesn't it make sense to use it to coat the lamb?

Start the recipe a day ahead to give the bread time to dry out and to allow the seasonings to permeate the lamb.

SERVES 8

**FOR THE LAMB**

1 teaspoon (6 g) fine sea salt

1½ teaspoons (3 g) toasted and crushed cumin seeds

Seeds from 15 green cardamom pods, crushed in a pestle

¼ teaspoon (0.5 g) freshly ground white or black pepper

One 4-pound (2-kg) boneless leg of lamb, rolled and tied

3 tablespoons (45 ml) grapeseed or other vegetable oil

**FOR THE BEANS AND BREAD**

1 cup (200 g) large dried white beans (I like Soissons or Cocos de Paimpol, but cannellini work well too) or two 16-ounce (454-g) cans white beans

1 loaf Poilâne-Style Sourdough (page 50) or other round sourdough

1 large egg, lightly beaten

**FOR THE VEGETABLES**

1 medium zucchini, chopped into ½-inch (1.25-cm) pieces

½ cup (70 g) frozen peas, thawed

¼ cup (30 g) hazelnuts, toasted, skinned, and coarsely chopped

½ preserved lemon, cut into ½-inch (1.25-cm) pieces

3 tablespoons (45 ml) grapeseed or other vegetable oil

¼ cup (60 ml) water

**THE DAY BEFORE SERVING, SEASON THE LAMB:** Combine the salt, cumin, cardamom, and pepper in a small bowl. Coat the lamb with the oil and sprinkle evenly with the spice mix, using your hands to ensure the lamb is well coated. Wrap with plastic wrap and refrigerate overnight.

**MEANWHILE, PREPARE THE BEANS AND BREAD:** If using dried beans, place them in a medium bowl and add enough cold water to cover them by 4 inches (10 cm). Soak the beans overnight.

Using a serrated bread knife, slice off the top of the loaf of bread; reserve it. Hollow out the loaf, leaving a 1½-inch (3.75-cm)-thick shell; reserve the bread you remove. Tear the bread into pieces and set aside overnight to dry. Wrap the bread shell and the top in plastic wrap and set aside.

The next day, drain the soaked beans and transfer them to a medium saucepan. Add enough water to cover by 1 inch (2.5 cm) and bring to a boil over high heat. Lower the heat and simmer the beans until barely tender, about 1 hour. Drain and set aside. (Or, if using canned beans, rinse and drain thoroughly; set aside.)

**ROAST THE LAMB:** Preheat the oven to 400°F (200°C). Set a rack in a roasting pan.

Process the bread you removed from the inside of the loaf in a food processor to fine crumbs. Spread half of the bread crumbs evenly on a large plate; reserve the rest for another use. Remove the lamb from the refrigerator, brush with the beaten egg, and coat evenly with the bread crumbs.

Transfer the lamb to the rack in the roasting pan and roast for 30 minutes.

Reduce the oven temperature to 350°F (180°C) and continue roasting until an instant-read thermometer inserted in the center of the lamb reads 125°F (51°C) for rare or 130°F (54°C) for medium-rare, 1 to 1½ hours; begin checking early.

**MEANWHILE, COOK THE VEGETABLES:** Scatter the zucchini over the bottom of the hollowed-out bread shell. Add the beans, peas, hazelnuts, and preserved lemon. Drizzle with the oil and water, then place the top back on the shell. Wrap in aluminum foil or parchment paper and bake for 45 minutes.

Remove the lamb from the oven and let rest for 10 minutes. Remove the vegetables en croûte and leave in the foil to keep warm.

Slice the lamb and transfer to a platter or plates. Remove the foil from the bread and present it, top off, at the table along with the lamb. Scoop out the vegetables to serve, then slice the bowl to serve some of the bread too.

# Sweet Potato and Sunchoke Stuffing

This is not like a typical American stuffing, but, then again, I live in Paris! While it includes bread (of course), it's used more to unite the vegetables than as a base. Indeed, as the stuffing soaks up the stock, it becomes almost creamy.

Sunchokes, also called Jerusalem artichokes, have a lovely nutty sweetness to them. Juniper is the main seasoning; its piney aroma plays well with the hearty vegetables and echoes a fall walk through the woods.

SERVES 8 TO 10

¼ cup (60 ml) extra-virgin olive oil

4 tablespoons (2 ounces; 57 g) unsalted butter

2 large onions, chopped into ¾-inch (2-cm) pieces

1 large sweet potato, peeled and chopped into ¾-inch (2-cm) pieces

4 small red-skinned potatoes, peeled and chopped into ¾-inch (2-cm) pieces

4 sunchokes, peeled and chopped into ¾-inch (2-cm) pieces

2 bay leaves, preferably fresh

Fine sea salt

¾ cup (180 ml) dry white wine

¾ cup (180 ml) water

1 teaspoon (1.5 g) ground juniper berries

2 large eggs

1 cup (240 ml) vegetable stock

1 pound (450 g) day-old bread, preferably with nuts and/or dried fruit, such as Rye Loaf with Currants (page 60), cut into ¾-inch (2-cm) cubes (about 8 cups)

½ cup (88 g) dried currants (unless there are currants in the bread)

Preheat the oven to 350°F (180°C). Butter a 9-by-13-inch (23-by-33-cm) baking dish.

In a large saucepan or a Dutch oven, heat the oil and butter over medium-high heat until the butter melts. Add the onions, sweet potato, red-skinned potatoes, sunchokes, bay leaves, and 1½ teaspoons salt and cook, stirring occasionally, until the onions soften, about 8 minutes. Pour in the wine and water and bring to a boil. Cook, stirring occasionally, until the potatoes are almost tender and most of the liquid is absorbed, about 10 minutes. Stir in the juniper and season to taste with salt. Remove from the heat and let cool slightly. Fish out the bay leaves and discard.

In a large bowl, whisk together the eggs and vegetable stock. Add the vegetable mixture and bread and stir and toss to combine. Stir in the currants, if using.

Transfer to the baking dish and bake, uncovered, until the top is golden and the edges are crisp, 45 minutes to 1 hour. Serve warm or at room temperature.

# The Art of Keeping Bread

WHEN I WAS GROWING UP, MY FAMILY HAD A SUNDAY NIGHT RITUAL: TAKING AN INVENTORY OF THE KITCHEN'S LEFTOVERS. Inevitably, they included bread and cheese. We would toast leftover bread slices, melt bits of cheese for a topping, and sprinkle a bit of cumin over the cheese. This is something I still love to do. It never fails to remind me of a quote from the French chemist Antoine Lavoisier: "Nothing is lost, nothing is created, everything is transformed."

At Poilâne, we try to close the shop each night with as little left over as possible. Our policy of baking throughout the day and staying attuned to our customers' needs helps us to adjust the production of breads, pastries, and cookies as needed and is an important part of our bakery's ethos. Whatever has not been sold when the shop closes is shared among colleagues.

If you're worried about your ability to eat the whole loaf of bread you bought, my first suggestion is to share it with friends, neighbors, or colleagues—especially if the bread in question is one of our huge sourdough loaves. In fact, the word *companion* stems from the Old French *compaignon*, meaning "one who breaks bread with another," from the Latin *com*, "with," and *panis*, "bread."

That said, our breads, especially our sourdough, keep well for several days, or even up to a week, the sour tang mellowing a bit over time. One reason is the sheer size of the loaf: It takes more time for a large loaf of bread to dry out than, say, a roll. The thick, almost caramelized crust also helps the loaf stay fresh.

A few summers back, I took a loaf of our wheat sourdough with me to Brittany on holiday with friends. We enjoyed the bread—in one form or another—for eleven days! At the start of vacation, we slathered soft sea-salted butter on fresh slices; on the last day, I turned the remainder of it into crumbs to coat fillets of freshly caught fish. Which brings us to the art of keeping bread—how best to store it and to appreciate a loaf's different phases as it ages. The simple recipes here are intended to show you how to use up every bit of bread.

# HOW TO STORE AND REFRESH BREAD

A product of fermentation, bread continues to react to its environment. It ages in one of two ways, either drying out or decomposing with humidity. Temperature and humidity are the variables to consider when storing your loaves. Extreme heat or cold accelerates drying. Therefore, moderate temperatures, from 59°F to 77°C (15°C to 25°C), are best for storage. A little humidity can slow the drying of bread, but too much can foster the growth of mold. The paper bags we sell our bread in are good for storage, because paper breathes; a linen or cotton cloth or bag has the same effect. We sell a cloth bag sized to hold our large sourdough; you can find smaller bags online (see Sources, page 277). In very dry environments, take the advice from a friend of mine who lives in the mountains: Put the bread in a paper bag, then in a plastic bag. The plastic keeps the humidity contained while the paper allows the loaf to breathe. Be sure to open the bag at least once daily—while you are cutting your slices, for example—to refresh the air inside.

In extremely humid conditions, the refrigerator can come in handy, providing a drier environment. In that case, check on the paper or linen bag daily to ensure there's not too much condensation forming. When I refrigerate bread, I wrap it in paper (or cloth) and then plastic so it does not pick up odors from other items.

Many Poilâne customers, especially those who purchase loaves via mail-order, freeze our breads. The trick is to freeze a loaf whole or in pieces as large as possible, to expose less of the surface to air. Wrap it tightly, ideally in the paper bag it came in, and then in an airtight plastic bag. Frozen this way, bread will keep for up to 3 months. To thaw, you have only one option: the kitchen counter and time. Never use a microwave or oven to defrost bread, since that can produce a rubbery crust.

For the short term, freezing individual slices is highly efficient and can be a breakfast savior. Wrap the slices in the paper bag, then in a plastic freezer bag. If you can, slip a piece of parchment paper between each slice so you can remove individual pieces more easily. Seal the bag, removing as much air as possible, and freeze. Frozen slices can be popped directly into a toaster. Since the slice will rehydrate as it defrosts in the toaster, you will likely need to pop it down a second time to properly brown it.

## HOW TO SLICE A GIANT SOURDOUGH
## (AND SMALLER LOAVES TOO)

Because of its size and thick crust, our sourdough can be a little intimidating to slice. First and most important, you must use a sharp serrated knife. Length is not as important as the serration; the knife's teeth need to be able to catch the crust and not slide over it into unplanned territory (like your fingers!).

Set the loaf on a large cutting board or wooden counter (the wood will keep the loaf from slipping as you slice). Holding the loaf an arm's length away, stand it straight up on one of its rounded edges, with the top of the loaf facing away, and cut it into two even halves, moving your hand as needed to hold the halves together as you cut. Remain your full arm's length away as you slice; this helps you make a straight cut and maintain a better grip. If you want longer slices for, say, tartines, lay a half down on its bottom and use a sawing motion to cut long slices starting from the cut side. For smaller sizes, place the half cut side down on the wood surface and slice down from one side to the other. The small end slices are best used for croutons.

# THE FOUR STAGES OF FRESHNESS

I classify the stages bread passes through as ultra-fresh, fresh, dry, and stale. Here's how to leave no crumb behind:

**ULTRA-FRESH:** If you stop by Poilâne during the last hour before closing, you can buy a loaf of bread from the very last batch baked that day. My friends tell me they often tear off pieces of the still-warm bread as they head home to enjoy it at its best. My favorite way to eat ultra-fresh bread is to cut a thick slice and spread it with some cultured butter. Bread this fresh also lends itself well to recipes that rely on its elasticity, such as Tenzin's Bread Maki (page 146).

**FRESH:** Bread that's a day or two old is easier to slice because it is slightly drier, making it perfect for tartines. With some of its moisture gone, fresh bread is also easier to process to crumbs in a blender when making recipes like gazpacho (page 121). A French artist, Pétra Werlé, who sculpts figurines made out of bread, inspired my recipe for a tart shell (page 224) that uses fresh bread crumbs to make a crust that doesn't need to be baked before being filled.

**DRY:** After 3 to 4 days, bread becomes dry. At this stage, the bread can still be refreshed by spraying it with a little bit of water and warming it for a few minutes directly on a rack in a 350°F (180°C) oven. But dry bread is good for making pain perdu (page 97 or 144) or pesto (page 165). Because it's easy to slice thin, it's also perfect for making bread chips (page 182).

**STALE:** Stale bread is best used for croutons or bread crumbs.

To make croutons from stale bread, remove the crust, then cut the crumb into the size you prefer. Let the bread continue to dry in a single layer, uncovered, until quite hard, about 6 to 8 hours. Once dried, the croutons can be stored in an airtight container at room temperature for a couple of days or frozen for a month or so. Plain croutons made from stale bread are not so tasty on their own in salads; they're meant to be used in preparations like stuffing (page 172), in which they will absorb flavorful juices. For more on other styles of croutons, see page 184. Stale bread also makes the best dry crumbs (reminiscent of Japanese panko), which are a great coating for meat (see page 170) or fish.

# Bread Crumbs

Due to the nature of my life and work, I'm never without bread crumbs or the ability to make some at a moment's notice. On the savory side, bread crumbs lighten a meatloaf (page 169) and create a crisp crust for lamb (page 170), or make a toasty topping for a vegetable gratin (page 147). On the sweet side, they replace ground nuts in my financiers, add crunch to ice cream, and flavor whipped cream. I make crumbs from all of our breads, including Black Pepper Pain de Mie (page 64) and Brioche (page 91). Simply process pieces of stale bread to the consistency you like or the recipe calls for. If your bread is not already dry, cut it into pieces, place it on a baking sheet, and bake in a 350°F (180°C) oven, tossing once or twice, until dry but not browned, 5 to 10 minutes. For most breads, you can leave the crust on, but our sourdough crust can be hard to process, so you may want to remove it or just leave a very little bit to get some of its deep, dark flavor. I often flavor crumbs with herbs and spices to give my dishes an extra boost of flavor, as in the Winter Vegetable Crumble with Citrus Bread Crumbs (page 166).

Well-dried crumbs will keep covered at room temperature for a couple of weeks, and they also freeze well, so you don't need to have something specific in mind to make them whenever you have excess bread.

# Bread Chips

Melba toasts, thin crisps of toast, were created by none other than Auguste Escoffier for the Australian opera singer whose stage name was Nellie Melba. (Peach Melba, also created by Escoffier, is named for her too.) These bread chips are similar to Melba toasts but a little less fussy. Perfect for all kinds of dips or to dunk into hot soup, they can be easily flavored with a sprinkling of fresh herbs—I especially like finely chopped rosemary—or by using a flavored oil or rubbing the dried slices with a clove of garlic. (If you will be using them for the Chocolate-Covered Bread Chips on page 236, however, keep them plain.) What follows is more of a guideline than a recipe, so how much you make is up to you.

Poilâne-Style Sourdough (page 50), Rye Bread (page 59), or Rye Loaf with Currants (page 60), very thinly sliced

Extra-virgin olive oil

Preheat the oven to 250°F (120°C). Line a baking sheet with parchment paper.

Spread out the bread slices in a single layer on the baking sheet. Drizzle lightly with oil. Bake, flipping once, until dry and cracker-like, 30 to 45 minutes (the timing will vary depending on thickness). Let cool, then break into pieces the size you like. The bread chips will keep in an airtight container at room temperature for 2 to 3 weeks.

# Croutons

If you have bread on hand, especially bread that's past its prime, there's no reason to ever buy croutons. On page 180, I describe the most basic kind, made from bread that's become so dry that it's crisp. But croutons can also be made "on demand" by toasting bread in the oven or frying it on the stove. It's best to use bread that's at least a few days old, since it's easier to slice.

For the most basic croutons, cut or tear the bread—crust on or off is up to you—into pieces the size you prefer. Spread the pieces on a rimmed baking sheet and let dry for a couple of days at room temperature, or toast in a low oven until crisp.

These unflavored croutons are best for preparations in which the bread will absorb flavors, such as a stuffing. If you want a crouton with more flavor to, say, perk up a green salad, fry the pieces in a little olive oil or butter on the stovetop until golden brown and season with salt and pepper. Alternatively, toss the bread with oil or melted butter and bake in a hot oven. If you want to flavor them further, you can toss with some spices or dried herbs before toasting. (If I am going to add fresh herbs or whole garlic cloves, I toss the croutons with them after toasting; remove the garlic before using.) Once cooled, the croutons will keep in an airtight container at room temperature for a couple of days. They can be frozen for up to 1 month.

# Croutons with Spirulina

Made from micro-algae, nutrient-dense spirulina powder has a strong, savory of-the-sea flavor (look for it in health food stores). I use just enough in these croutons to turn them a blue-green color. They are a great snack with drinks.

MAKES 4 CUPS

1 tablespoon (7 g) spirulina powder (see headnote)

1 cup (240 ml) hot water

2 tablespoons (30 ml) extra-virgin olive oil

2 tablespoons (1 ounce; 28 g) unsalted butter

8 ounces (227 g) day-old Poilâne-Style Sourdough (page 50), cut into ¾-inch (2-cm) pieces (about 4 cups)

Line a baking sheet with paper towels. In a small bowl, whisk the spirulina and water together until the spirulina is dissolved.

In a large skillet, combine the olive oil and butter and heat over medium heat until the butter is melted. Dip the bread cubes quickly one by one in the spirulina water, then add to the pan. Fry, turning occasionally, until they are toasted and crisp on all sides, 7 to 10 minutes. Transfer to the paper towel–lined baking sheet to drain briefly. Serve warm.

# Dukkah Croutons

Coating large croutons in dukkah—an Egyptian nut and spice mix—imbues them with its fragrance and makes them an irresistible snack or a wonderful addition to salads, including the beet salad on page 126.

MAKES 4 CUPS

¼ cup (40 g) pistachios

1 tablespoon (9 g) sesame seeds

1 teaspoon (2 g) cumin seeds

1 teaspoon (2 g) coriander seeds

½ teaspoon (2 pinches; 1 g) dried mint (optional)

½ teaspoon (3 g) fine sea salt

¼ teaspoon (2 large pinches; 0.5 g) freshly ground black pepper

5 tablespoons (75 ml) extra-virgin olive oil

8 ounces (227 g) day-old Poilâne-Style Sourdough (page 50), cut into ¾-inch (2-cm) pieces (about 4 cups)

In a food processor, combine the pistachios, sesame seeds, cumin, coriander, mint, if using, salt, and pepper and pulse to make a coarse spice mix. Or crush in a mortar with the pestle.

Heat ¼ cup (60 ml) of the oil in a large skillet over medium-high heat. Add the bread cubes and fry, turning occasionally, until golden brown, about 5 minutes. Add the spice mixture and the remaining 1 tablespoon (15 ml) oil and cook, stirring, for another minute, until the croutons are toasted, golden, and crisp on all sides, another 1 to 2 minutes.

Remove from the heat and serve warm or cool completely. The croutons can be stored in an airtight container at room temperature for a day or two.

# Sweets

AFTER LUNCH AT HOME, I HEAD BACK TO THE BAKERY TO WORK IN MY OFFICE. Throughout the afternoon, the scents from cakes and cookies waft up the stairwell, reminding me that I will soon need a little pick-me-up.

In Paris, pâtisseries specialize in pastries and cakes, while boulangeries focus on breads. Poilâne is a boulangerie, but we do offer some sweet baked goods. We stick to just a few simple, comforting pastries that are made in our wood-fired ovens. I call them *pâtisseries boulangères*. What sets them apart from those you'll find at a typical pâtisserie is that they are less sweet. Our apple tarts, for example, have no sugar in the dough or filling, save for a little brown sugar sprinkled on top after baking. Punitions, our famous butter cookies, have just enough sweetness to entice you to eat another.

We often put a basket of punitions right by the register in each of our shops for customers to nibble on while they wait. When I was little, I would walk down the line of customers on busy days, distributing cookies. You could also find me in the back room, under my grandfather's careful watch, packing bags of them in various weights; he taught me both to be careful and to be generous, adding more than promised. His spirit still imbues the bakery, and when we package our punitions today, we always add extra.

The other pâtisseries boulangères we sell are made from puff pastry (*pâte feuilletée*). Like croissant dough, it gets its many layers when the dough is repeatedly folded around butter. When the pastry is baked, the heat from the oven turns the water in the butter into steam, which forces the sheets of dough and butter apart, resulting in the flaky texture.

The secret to puff pastry lies in the number of folds: Too few make a plump, uninteresting texture; too many produce lots of layers but are too dry. I like to think we make ours just right. We use puff pastry to make apple tarts, turnovers, custard cakes, and, during the holidays, *galettes des rois* (kings' cakes).

Because I am a lazy baker at home, I use bread in desserts. Not only does the bread speed things up, it also adds flavor and texture. In a delicious twist on *baba au rhum*, instead of making the traditional yeasted sponge cake, I soak brioche in a lemony rum syrup and flambé it. I've also found that bread makes an almost instant yet delicious tart shell.

The recipes in this chapter include some of the pastries we bake at Poilâne as well as the simple confections I make at home.

# Punitions

Made with just five basic ingredients, these cookies are the simplest of our offerings and among the most beloved. Based on a cookie from Normandy, they're from the same recipe my great-great-grandmother used to bake for her grandchildren. She would call them to come collect their *punitions*, or "punishments." When they ran to her, she would smile widely and open her hand to reveal these small, thin, scalloped-edge treats. They can be topped with jam or dunked into a hot drink.

The punitions at Poilâne range in color from light to quite dark. The cookies baked longer get darker, and the variation in appearance and flavor is part of their charm. I'm fascinated to see the different tastes our clients have as they reach with purpose for a light golden cookie, one with just the edges darkened a bit, or one baked until *bien cuit* ("well done"). Those are my favorite too, because I love their deep caramelized flavor. If you'd like a range of doneness, don't turn the pans during baking, so the cookies bake a little unevenly. You can also leave one sheet in the oven longer than the other.

MAKES ABOUT SEVENTY 2-INCH (5-CM) COOKIES

2 sticks (8 ounces; 227 g) unsalted butter, preferably cultured (see page 76), cubed, softened

1⅓ cups (264 g) sugar

¼ teaspoon (1.5 g) fine sea salt

1 large egg plus 1 large egg yolk, at room temperature

490 g (3½ cups) all-purpose flour, plus more for dusting

Using a hand mixer on medium-high speed, combine the butter, sugar, and salt in a large bowl and mix until light and fluffy, 2 to 3 minutes. Add the egg and yolk and mix until just combined. Gradually add the flour, mixing just until a dough forms. Alternatively, mix by hand in a large bowl or directly on a work surface as shown on pages 194 and 195.

Divide the dough in half and form into 2 disks. Wrap each in plastic wrap and refrigerate for at least 30 minutes, and up to 2 days.

Position racks in the upper and lower thirds and preheat the oven to 350°F (180°C). Line two baking sheets with parchment paper.

Lightly flour a work surface. Using a lightly floured rolling pin, roll the dough out one piece at a time to a thickness of ⅛ inch (0.33 cm). Cut out rounds using a 2-inch (5-cm) round cookie cutter, preferably fluted, and place the rounds ½ inch (1.25 cm) apart on the baking sheets. (See the photos on page 194 and 195.)

Bake until the centers of the cookies are set, 12 to 15 minutes, or longer if you like them darker. If you prefer the cookies uniformly baked, rotate the pans from top to bottom and front to back halfway through the baking time. Immediately transfer the cookies to a wire rack and let cool completely. Store the cookies in an airtight container at room temperature for up to a week.

# Berry Crumble with Punitions

Rich, buttery punitions complement tart fruit in this rustic crumble made by combining the fruit with crushed cookies. Instead of sprinkling the crumbs on top, as with a traditional topping, I add the cookies directly to the berries, making the dessert almost cake-like. Try this with a single berry or a mix, depending on what looks best at the market.

SERVES 6 TO 8

3 cups (425 g) berries, preferably a mix, such as blueberries, blackberries, and raspberries

1½ teaspoons (4 g) cornstarch

3 or 4 drops orange blossom water or rose water (optional)

5½ ounces (158 g) Punitions (page 193; about 24 cookies) or your favorite butter cookie or shortbread, crushed (1½ cups)

Fine sea salt

Heavy cream, ice cream, or crème fraîche, for serving

Position a rack in the middle and preheat the oven to 325°F (160°C).

Put 1 cup (142 g) of the berries in a large bowl and use a rubber spatula or wooden spoon to crush them slightly. Add the cornstarch and orange blossom or rose water, if using, and mix to combine. Add the remaining whole berries, the cookies, and a pinch of salt and stir just to combine.

Using a spatula, scrape the mixture into an 8- or 9-inch (20- or 23-cm) round cake pan and smooth the top. Bake until set, golden, and fragrant, about 45 minutes. Let cool slightly on a wire rack.

Serve warm or at room temperature, topped with cream, ice cream, or crème fraîche.

# Chocolate Truffles

Crushed butter cookies add texture to these chocolate truffles both inside and as a coating. You can add other flavorings, such as ground coffee, cardamom, or even a pinch of ground chile, with the cookie crumbs if you like.

MAKES ABOUT 30 TRUFFLES

6 ounces (175 g) 70% to 80% dark chocolate, finely chopped

½ cup (120 ml) heavy cream

3 tablespoons (1½ ounces; 42 g) salted butter, cubed, softened

9 ounces (250 g) Punitions (page 193; about 40 cookies) or your favorite butter cookie or shortbread, coarsely crushed (2 cups)

Unsweetened cocoa powder, for dusting

Place the chocolate in a medium bowl.

In a small saucepan over medium-high heat, bring the cream just to a boil. Immediately remove from the heat and pour over the chocolate. Whisk gently until the chocolate is melted and smooth (for an extremely smooth mixture, use an immersion blender). Gradually stir in the butter until melted. Fold in ½ cup (62 g) of the crushed cookies. Cover the bowl with plastic wrap and refrigerate for at least 3 hours, and up to overnight.

Finely crush the remaining cookies. Place the crumbs in a large shallow bowl. Using your hands, form the chocolate mixture into 1½-inch (3.75-cm) balls and roll in the cookie crumbs. Dust with cocoa powder. Serve immediately, or refrigerate for up to 5 days in an airtight container.

# Forgive-Me Biscuits

I created these treats as an apology to my vacation-rental neighbors after my dog, missing me while I was out for dinner, spent a good few hours howling. Since I knew my neighbors loved my dog, I also wanted to make something for them that could be shared with a furry friend.

Instead of sugar, the cookies are sweetened with a dried fruit puree. As you probably know, the French, like the English, call cookies "biscuits." In this case, the name is apt.

MAKES 12 TO 15 LARGE COOKIES

| | |
|---|---|
| ⅓ cup (60 g) dried currants | 125 g (1 cup) oat flour |
| ½ cup (120 ml) coconut oil | 25 g (2 tablespoons) all-purpose flour |
| 1 tablespoon (15 ml) plain yogurt, any style (Greek-style yogurt will yield denser cookies) | ¼ cup (22.5 g) old-fashioned rolled oats |

Place the currants in a bowl, add enough water to cover, and soak for at least 1 hour, and up to 3 hours.

Position a rack in the middle and preheat the oven to 350°F (180°C). Line a baking sheet with parchment paper.

Drain the currants and transfer them to a blender. Add the coconut oil and blend until pureed. Add the yogurt and blend until combined.

In a medium bowl, mix together both flours and the rolled oats. Add the currant puree and mix until thoroughly combined.

Drop heaping teaspoons of the dough onto the prepared baking sheet, leaving at least 1 inch (2.5 cm) between them. Bake until the cookies are lightly browned, about 15 minutes. Transfer to a wire rack to cool. Store in an airtight container at room temperature for up to 3 days.

# Puff Pastry (Pâte Feuilletée)

This classic pâte feuilleté is a building block for many of our sweets. Literally translated, the name means "flaky pastry." Though straightforward, puff pastry takes a few, albeit mostly hands-off, hours to make because after you roll out the dough each time and fold it over itself to make multiple layers, a process known as a "turn," it needs to rest for at least a half hour to let the gluten relax (which also makes rolling easier).

We use puff pastry for our Apple Tarts (page 204), Custard Tart, and Galettes des Rois (pages 208 and 211).

MAKES 1½ POUNDS (680 G)

| | |
|---|---|
| 315 g (2¼ cups) all-purpose flour, plus more for dusting | ⅔ cup (160 ml) ice-cold water |
| ½ teaspoon (3 g) fine sea salt | 2 sticks (8 ounces; 227 g) unsalted butter, slightly softened |

In a large bowl, combine 280 g (2 cups) of the flour and the salt. Gradually add the water and mix gently with your hands until a rough dough forms; the dough will be shaggy and sticky, which is fine. Form the dough into a ball, wrap in plastic, and refrigerate for at least 1 hour and up to 2 days.

Meanwhile, in the bowl of a stand mixer fitted with the paddle attachment, beat the butter on medium speed until smooth. Add the remaining 35 g (¼ cup) flour and mix until smooth. Scrape the butter onto a piece of plastic wrap and shape into a 5-inch (13-cm) square. Wrap well in the plastic and refrigerate for 30 minutes.

Lightly flour a work surface. Transfer the dough to the surface and roll into a 9-inch (23-cm) square. Position the butter block on the dough square so that each corner of the butter block points at the middle of one side of the dough. Gently pulling on one corner of the dough, lift and stretch the flap over the butter block until it just reaches the center of the block. Repeat with the other corners of the dough to completely envelop the butter, then pinch the seams together to seal in the butter.

Turn the dough so it's seam side down and reshape it with your hands as necessary so its sides are straight. Roll out the dough into a 14-by-7-inch (35-by-17-cm) rectangle. With a long side facing you, fold one third of the dough over the middle, then fold the other third over, as if you're folding a business letter. Wrap in plastic wrap and refrigerate for 30 minutes.

For the first turn, remove the dough from the refrigerator and roll out again into a 14-by-7-inch (35-by-17-cm) rectangle. Fold like a letter as described in the previous step and refrigerate for 30 minutes to 1 hour.

Repeat this step two more times, refrigerating the dough for 30 minutes to 1 hour each time, for a total of 3 turns. Wrap the dough well in plastic wrap and refrigerate for at least 2 hours, and ideally overnight, before using.

The dough can be refrigerated for 2 days or frozen, well wrapped, for up to 2 months. Thaw frozen dough overnight in the refrigerator before using.

# Apple Tarts

My grandfather grew up in Normandy, which has an abundance of apples. Many of the region's pastries feature the fruit. In our apple tarts, we use the Golden Delicious variety. To make the tarts, a few thick apple slices are arranged on a square of puff pastry, then the edges of the dough are folded over the fruit and baked. The brown sugar sprinkled over the still-hot tarts melts a bit and adds a subtle sweetness. The tarts are best warm from the oven, but also delicious at room temperature.

MAKES 8 INDIVIDUAL TARTS

All-purpose flour, for dusting

1 recipe Puff Pastry (page 202) or 1½ pounds (680 g) other all-butter puff pastry

4 medium Golden Delicious or Granny Smith apples, peeled, cored, and cut into ½-inch (1.25-cm)-thick wedges

1 large egg, beaten with 1 tablespoon (15 ml) water for egg wash

Scant 3 tablespoons (44.75 g) dark brown sugar

Fine sea salt

Line two baking sheets with parchment paper. Lightly flour a work surface. Roll out the puff pastry to a rectangle slightly larger than 11½ by 22 inches (29 by 56 cm).

Using a sharp knife or pizza cutter, trim the dough to make the corners square. Cut the dough in half, then cut each half into 4 squares. You will have eight 5½-inch (14-cm) squares. Lightly roll each square to thin it a little. Place the squares on the baking sheets, leaving ample space between them. (See page 207 for how to use the scraps.)

Arrange 3 apple wedges in the middle of one square, points touching, so their rounded sides face out and their straight sides face in, leaving a border of bare dough all around; the inside of the joined slices should look like a triangle, the outside like a circle. Working your way around the square, stretch the dough up over the apples, folding and pleating it as you go as necessary, leaving the center of the tart open; strive for 8 to 12 pleats. Cut a fourth apple wedge in half and place the piece in the middle of the tart. Repeat with the remaining dough and apples. Refrigerate for at least 30 minutes, and up to a few hours, before baking.

Position racks in the middle and lower thirds and preheat the oven to 400°F (200°C).

Using a pastry brush, brush the crusts of the tarts with the egg wash. Bake, rotating the pans from top to bottom and front to back halfway through, until the puff pastry is golden and the apples are soft, 35 to 45 minutes. Immediately sprinkle each tart with about a teaspoon of the brown sugar and a pinch of sea salt; don't worry if the sugar does

continued

not melt. Let cool slightly on a wire rack before serving.

These tarts are best enjoyed the day they're made but can be gently reheated the next day: Preheat the oven to 350°F (180°C), then turn off the heat. Put the tarts in the hot oven with the door propped slightly ajar for about 7 minutes.

## Variation

To make a single large tart, shown below, use half of the rolled-out dough. With a sharp paring knife, cut a 12-inch (30-cm) circle out of the dough (use a plate or a pan lid as a guide) and transfer it to a parchment-lined baking sheet. Fill the center with the apple slices, using all of them: Pile the slices—there's no need to be fussy—on the dough, leaving a 2-inch (5-cm) border all around. Fold the edges of the dough up and over the apples, pleating as you go. Increase the baking time by 45 to 55 minutes. Serves 6.

# ARLETTES
# (CINNAMON-SUGAR COOKIES)

Chances are you will have a little leftover puff pastry when making the recipes in this chapter. I hate waste, so I use the scraps to make arlettes, which are crisp, wafer-thin cinnamon-sugar cookies; baking them essentially caramelizes the sugar in puff pastry. Sounds good, no?

Whisk together ¼ cup (30 g) confectioners' sugar and 1 tablespoon (8 g) ground cinnamon. Gather your puff pastry scraps and roll them out into a ⅛-inch (0.3 cm)-thick rectangle. Sprinkle it all over with some of the cinnamon-sugar mixture; you want a nice light coating. Using gentle pressure, starting from a short side of the rectangle, roll up the dough into a tight log. Freeze briefly to firm it up, then cut into slices about ⅓ inch (0.8 cm) thick. Using the rolling pin, roll out each slice into a thin oval. Transfer the ovals to a parchment-lined baking sheet. Beat an egg with a little water. Brush the egg wash onto the arlettes and sprinkle with more cinnamon sugar. Bake at 375°F (190°C) until golden brown on the edges, 15 to 20 minutes.

# Galette des Rois

Galette des rois ("kings' cake") is a classic French dessert made to celebrate Epiphany (January 6). The celebration is said to be rooted in the ancient Roman festival Saturnalia, which celebrates Saturn, the god of the sun, and the cake's round shape suggests the sun. Galette des rois was originally made with two puff pastry rounds baked together, with a porcelain charm (*fève*) hidden inside. Whoever has the slice with the fève gets a paper crown (supplied when you purchase the cake at any French bakery). Traditionally, the youngest in the room is asked to sit under the table and name the person who should receive each slice—that way, no one can cheat to get the fève. Although my sister, Athena, was younger, I always kept her company under the table.

Nowadays most galettes des rois are filled with frangipane, but at Poilâne, we sell a hazelnut-cream version that's very popular (see page 211). I prefer the original style, with no filling, but you can take your choice. And you can decide whether or not to add a charm. Warn your guests if you do bake one into the galette.

My father used to organize galette parties for our grade-school classes, and I have fond memories of him coming into school with a huge galette and an equally huge grin. To this day, Athena and I always celebrate together at holiday time with this dessert.

MAKES ONE 10-INCH (25-CM) GALETTE;
SERVES 4 TO 6

All-purpose flour, for dusting

1 recipe Puff Pastry (page 202) or 1½ pounds (680 g) other all-butter puff pastry

1 large egg, beaten with 1 tablespoon (15 ml) water for egg wash

A whole hazelnut or almond, a large dried bean, or a ceramic galette des rois charm (optional)

1 tablespoon (7.5 g) confectioners' sugar

¼ teaspoon (0.7 g) ground cinnamon (optional)

1 tablespoon (15 ml) hot water

Line a baking sheet with parchment paper. Lightly flour a work surface. Cut the dough in half. Roll each half into an 11½-inch (29-cm) square, ⅛ inch (0.3 cm) thick. Use a sharp paring knife to cut out two 10-inch (25-cm) rounds, using a plate or a pan lid as a guide. (See page 207 for how to use the scraps.)

Transfer one of the rounds to the prepared baking sheet. Brush the edges of the round with some of the egg wash (try to avoid letting the egg wash drip down the edges, or it will inhibit the pastry from rising). If using a charm, press it into the dough, about 2 inches (5 cm) or so from one edge. Top the

*continued*

dough with the second round and press the edges together with your fingertips. Using the back of the paring knife, scallop the edges by pushing the knife into the dough ¼ to ½ inch (0.6 to 1.25 cm) deep every ½ inch (1.25 cm) or so. Then, again using the back of the paring knife, draw a decorative pattern, such as a diamond-shaped crosshatch, on top of the pastry without cutting into it. Cover with plastic wrap and refrigerate for 30 minutes. (Cover and refrigerate the remaining egg wash.)

Position a rack in the lower third and preheat the oven to 375°F (190°C).

Brush the top of the galette lightly with egg wash, again making sure it doesn't drip down the edge). Using the paring knife, cut 5 small slits in the top of the galette. Bake until the pastry is puffed and evenly browned, about 25 minutes.

Meanwhile, sift together the sugar and cinnamon, if using, into a small bowl; or just sift in the sugar. Whisk in the hot water to create a glaze.

Remove the galette from the oven, brush with the glaze, and return to the oven for 1 minute, or until the top is shiny. Serve warm. Store any leftovers, covered, at room temperature.

# Galette des Rois with Hazelnut Cream

While the original galette des rois was just two layers of puff pastry (see page 208), bakers eventually began to fill their kings' cakes with almond cream, which has now become the norm. Although my family prefers the plain one, my father knew that due to customer demand, we needed a filled one. In 1999, he created this hazelnut filling, which has since become a highly anticipated seasonal offering. Adding a charm (see headnote, page 208) is optional, but if you do, be sure to warn your guests to be on the lookout for it.

MAKES ONE 10-INCH (25-CM) GALETTE;
SERVES 4 TO 6

4 tablespoons (2 ounces; 57 g) unsalted butter, cut into pieces, softened

3 tablespoons (40 g) sugar

½ cup (70 g) hazelnuts, toasted, skinned, and finely ground in a food processor

1 large egg

All-purpose flour, for rolling

1 recipe Puff Pastry (page 202) or 1½ pounds (680 g) other all-butter puff pastry

A whole hazelnut or almond, a large dried bean, or a ceramic galette des rois charm (optional)

1 large egg, beaten with 1 tablespoon (15 ml) water for egg wash

In the bowl of a stand mixer fitted with the paddle attachment, beat the butter and sugar on medium-high speed until fluffy, 3 to 4 minutes. Add the ground hazelnuts and beat until well blended. Switch to the whisk attachment, add the egg, and whisk until well blended. (*The filling can be covered and refrigerated for up to 24 hours; bring to room temperature before using it.*)

Line a baking sheet with parchment paper. Lightly flour a work surface.

Cut the dough in half. Roll each half into an 11½-inch (29-cm) square, ⅛ inch (0.3 cm) thick. Use a sharp paring knife to cut out two 10-inch (25-cm) rounds, using a plate or pan lid as a guide. (See page 207 for how to use the scraps.)

Transfer one of the rounds to the prepared baking sheet. Leaving a 1-inch (2.5-cm) border, spread the filling evenly over the dough. Press the charm, if using, into the filling, about 2 inches (5 cm) or so from one edge. Moisten the border of the dough with egg wash (try to avoid letting the egg wash

continued

drip down the edges, or it will inhibit the pastry from rising). Position the second circle of dough over the filling and press the edges together with your fingertips to seal well. Using the back of the paring knife, scallop the edges by pushing the knife into the dough ¼ to ½ inch (0.6 to 1.25 cm) deep every ½ inch (1.25 cm) or so. Then, again using the back of the knife, draw a decorative pattern, such as a diamond-shaped crosshatch, on top of the galette without cutting into it. Cover with plastic wrap and refrigerate for 30 minutes. (Cover and refrigerate the remaining egg wash.)

Position a rack in the lower third and preheat the oven to 375°F (190°C).

Brush the top of the galette lightly with egg wash, again making sure it doesn't drip down the edges. Using the paring knife, cut 5 small slits in the top of the galette. Bake until the galette is puffed and evenly browned, about 25 minutes.

Serve warm. Store any leftovers covered at room temperature.

Custard Tart (French Flan; opposite)

# Custard Tart (French Flan)

If you know flan as the caramel-drenched Spanish dessert, it may surprise you that in France, *flan* is a creamy custard baked in a flaky crust. Our version, with a sunny filling and a textured surface caramelized in spots, is a bit unusual in that we don't add vanilla, as traditional recipes do. Instead, we use brown sugar, which deepens the flavor of the custard. Our customers often request a slice right out of the oven but consequently burn their tongues on the hot, still wobbly custard—flan is best cooled before slicing and serving.

MAKES ONE 9-INCH (23-CM) TART; SERVES 8

Unsalted butter, softened, for the pan

40 g (5 tablespoons) all-purpose flour, plus more for rolling

½ recipe Puff Pastry (page 202) or 12 ounces (336 g) other all-butter puff pastry

⅓ cup (40 g) cornstarch

3 large eggs

1 quart (950 ml) whole milk

¾ cup plus 2 tablespoons packed (180 g) light brown sugar

Butter a 9-inch (23-cm) round cake pan.

Lightly flour a work surface. Roll out the puff pastry to an 11½-inch (29-cm) square, about ⅛ inch (0.3 cm) thick. Use a sharp paring knife to cut out a 10-inch (25-cm) circle of dough, using a plate or a pan lid as a guide. (See page 207 for how to use the scraps.)

Gently transfer the dough to the prepared pan. Lift up the dough to provide enough slack so it lines the sides by about 1 inch (2.5 cm), without stretching the dough. With a fork, prick holes in the bottom of the dough to prevent air bubbles as it bakes. Cover with plastic wrap and refrigerate while you make the custard.

In a small bowl, whisk together the flour and cornstarch. In a medium bowl, lightly beat the eggs. Add the cornstarch-flour mixture to the eggs and mix well.

Heat the milk and brown sugar in a large saucepan over medium heat, stirring occasionally to dissolve the sugar, until you see large bubbles. Lower the heat to a simmer.

Gradually whisk about ¾ cup (180 ml) of the hot milk mixture into the egg mixture, then whisk this mixture back into the saucepan. Increase the heat to medium-high and cook, whisking vigorously, until large bubbles appear on the surface. Remove from the heat and immediately pour the custard into the chilled puff pastry shell. Let cool to room temperature, then cover loosely with plastic wrap and refrigerate for at least 1 hour, and up to 24 hours.

Position a rack in the lower third and preheat the oven to 425°F (220°C).

Bake the tart until the surface darkens in spots, 35 to 40 minutes. Let cool on a wire rack before slicing and serving. This tastes best the day it's made, but you can cover and refrigerate it for up to 2 days.

# Rye-Cocoa Cake

This is one of the most popular desserts at Comptoir Poilâne. I was inspired to pair rye flour and cocoa after breathing in the flour's earthy, floral aroma. The cake, which is very chocolaty, lies on the cusp of sweet and savory, just the way I prefer my treats.

MAKES ONE 9-BY-5-INCH (23-BY-13-CM) LOAF

Softened butter, for the pan

240 g (1¾ cups) rye flour

½ cup (40 g) unsweetened cocoa powder, preferably Dutch-processed

1 teaspoon (4 g) baking powder

1 teaspoon (6 g) fine sea salt

1 cup (240 ml) whole milk

¾ cup packed (160 g) light brown sugar

½ cup (120 ml) neutral oil, such as canola

½ cup (120 ml) extra-virgin olive oil

2 large eggs

Position a rack in the middle and preheat the oven to 350°F (180°C). Butter a 9-by-5-inch (23-by-13-cm) loaf pan and line it with parchment paper.

Sift together the flour, cocoa powder, baking powder, and salt into a medium bowl.

In a large bowl, whisk together the milk and brown sugar. Whisk in both oils and the eggs. Add the flour mixture and use a rubber spatula to stir it in until just combined. Transfer to the prepared pan.

Bake, rotating the pan halfway through, until the top is set and a knife inserted in the center of the loaf comes out clean, 30 to 35 minutes. Let cool completely on a wire rack before unmolding. Serve at room temperature.

Store the cake, covered, at room temperature for up to 5 days. Or wrap well in plastic wrap and foil and freeze for up to 3 months.

## JUST DON'T CALL THEM "QUICK BREADS"!

We call homey snack cakes *gâteaux de voyages,* which translates "travel cakes." The cakes, usually baked in a loaf pan, are sturdy, which means they will hold up when packed with a book and a bottle of water for a long train ride. Their simple, not-too-sweet flavor makes them perfect anytime, and they usually stay fresh at room temperature for a few days; some even improve in flavor.

Are they quick to make? They are indeed, but I think *gâteaux de voyage* is far more romantic than "quick bread." We serve these at the café and sell them at the bakery for customers who want a transportable treat.

# Carrot and Curry Cake

At college, a teaching fellow, who was also a passionate baker, brought to class some amazing cookies flavored with curry powder. Initially he refused to share the recipe—probably because he thought I'd steal his creation for Poilâne. I devoured them so quickly that he soon realized my motive was purely personal. He finally relented, and his secret is still safe with me.

I did, however, borrow the notion of including curry powder in sweets. In this cake, the curry is subtle and it perfectly complements the carrots as well as the maple syrup we use instead of sugar. A slice on its own is fantastic, but it's even more delicious toasted and slathered with cream cheese.

MAKES ONE 9-BY-5-INCH (23-BY-13-CM) LOAF

| | |
|---|---|
| Softened butter, for the pan | ⅔ cup (160 ml) pure maple syrup |
| 300 g (2 cups plus 2 tablespoons) rye flour | ¾ cup (180 ml) neutral oil, such as canola |
| 1 tablespoon (8 g) curry powder, such as Madras | ¼ cup (80 g) applesauce |
| 2 teaspoons (8 g) baking powder | 2½ cups (200 g) grated carrots (from about 4 large carrots) |
| 1 teaspoon (6 g) fine sea salt | ¼ cup (25 g) crushed walnuts |
| 3 large eggs | ¼ teaspoon (1 ml) orange blossom water (optional) |

Position a rack in the middle and preheat the oven to 350°F (180°C). Butter a 9-by-5-inch (23-by-13-cm) loaf pan and line with parchment paper.

In a large bowl, whisk together the flour, curry powder, baking powder, and salt.

In a medium bowl, whisk together the eggs and maple syrup. Slowly pour in the oil, whisking constantly, until combined. Whisk in the applesauce. Add the wet ingredients to the dry and fold them together with a rubber spatula just until combined. Gently stir in the carrots, walnuts, and orange blossom water, if using. Scrape into the prepared pan.

Bake, rotating the pan halfway through, until the top is golden brown and a toothpick inserted in the center comes out clean, 45 to 50 minutes. Let cool completely on a wire rack before unmolding.

Store the cake, covered, at room temperature for up to 5 days. Or wrap well in plastic wrap and foil and freeze for up to 3 months.

# Spice Cake

Since we're a family business, many of our suppliers have also been "in the family" for generations. But, as in life, nothing is set in stone. For a long time, we bought what we thought was the best spice cake to sell at our store, believing we could do the classic cake no better. Then, in 2010, our source stopped supplying.

What seemed like a curse became a blessing: It gave us a chance to explore the world of spice cake, or, as we French call it, *pain d'épices*, and create our own loaf. The cake is popular throughout Europe, and each capital (Dijon, Strasbourg, Basel, Brussels, and more) has developed its own blend. We enlisted the help of New York City–based spice blender Lior Lev Sercarz. You can order our mix online (see Sources, page 277), but feel free to play with different combinations to create your own; see the suggested blend below. The finished loaf, dense and heavily spiced, tastes even better a day or two after baking.

MAKES ONE 9-BY-5-INCH (23-BY-13-CM) LOAF

Softened butter, for the pan

325 g (2⅓ cups) all-purpose flour

1 teaspoon (5 g) baking soda

¾ cup packed (160 g) light brown sugar

¾ cup (180 ml) lukewarm water

½ cup (120 ml) honey, preferably wildflower honey

¼ cup (20 g) Apollonia N.29 spice blend by Lior Lev Sercarz (see Sources, page 277), or a mix of 2 teaspoons (4 g) ground ginger, ½ teaspoon (0.5 g) ground cinnamon, and a pinch ground cloves

½ teaspoon (3 g) fine sea salt

2 large eggs

Position a rack in the middle and preheat the oven to 350°F (180°C). Butter a 9-by-5-inch (23-by-13-cm) loaf pan and line the bottom with parchment paper.

In a medium bowl, whisk together the flour and baking soda.

In a large bowl, whisk together the brown sugar, water, honey, spices, and salt until the sugar dissolves. Add the eggs and whisk just until combined. Add the flour and baking soda and fold in with a rubber spatula just until combined. Pour into the pan.

Bake, rotating the pan halfway through, until the top is set and a knife or toothpick inserted in the center comes out clean, 40 to 45 minutes. Transfer the pan to a wire rack and let cool for 10 minutes before unmolding onto the rack. Turn right side up and let cool completely on the rack before slicing.

Store the cake, covered, at room temperature for up to 5 days. Or wrap well in plastic wrap and foil and freeze for up to 3 months.

# Croissant Pudding

Croissants are at their best the day they're made, but there's a limit to how many you can eat in one sitting! Give leftovers new life with this pudding and its four seasonal variations. Feel free to use oat milk (store-bought or homemade, page 261) or nut milk (my favorite is almond) in place of the whole milk, but in that case, add an extra egg to help bind the ingredients.

SERVES 6 TO 8

2 large eggs

½ cup packed (75 g) light brown sugar

Fine sea salt

2 cups (480 ml) whole milk (see headnote)

Six 1- to 2-day-old Croissants (page 81) or other all-butter croissants, torn into thirds

Softened butter, for the pan

Whipped cream, for serving

In a medium bowl, whisk together the eggs, brown sugar, and a pinch of salt. Pour in the milk and whisk until frothy.

Place the torn croissants in a large bowl and pour the egg mixture over them. Toss together and let sit at room temperature for 2 hours so the croissants absorb the liquid (or cover with plastic wrap and refrigerate overnight).

Position a rack in the middle and preheat the oven to 350°F (180°C). Butter an 8-inch (20-cm) square baking pan.

Transfer the croissant mixture, including any liquid, to the pan. Bake until the custard is set and the top is browned, 40 to 45 minutes. Let cool slightly on a wire rack.

Cut the pudding into slices and serve warm or cold with whipped cream, if you like.

## Seasonal Variations

For each variation, toss the ingredients with the torn croissants before adding the milk mixture. If you like, nestle the fruit decoratively among the croissants before baking.

### SPRING (see photograph)

1 pint (340 g) strawberries, hulled and chopped

2 teaspoons (1 g) finely chopped fresh tarragon

*continued*

SUMMER (see photograph)

2 ripe medium peaches or nectarines, halved, pitted, and chopped or sliced

1 tablespoon (15 ml) Lillet Blanc or dry vermouth

1½ teaspoons (0.75 g) finely chopped fresh rosemary

WINTER

2 cups (227 g) mixed citrus segments (such as orange, grapefruit, and lemon), chopped

1 tablespoon (10 g) chopped candied ginger

¼ teaspoon (large pinch; 0.5 g) ground cardamom

FALL

2 very ripe persimmons, chopped

1 cup (100 g) vacuum-packed or jarred whole peeled roasted chestnuts, chopped

¼ teaspoon (1 ml) pure vanilla extract

¼ teaspoon (large pinch; 0.5 g) freshly ground black pepper

# Chocolate Ganache Tart with Walnut-Date Bread Crust

This no-bake tart crust is made of bread crumbs and chopped dates. Be sure to give the crust time to firm up in the refrigerator so you will be able to slice the tart easily.

MAKES ONE 9-INCH (23-CM) TART

**FOR THE CRUST**

4 ounces (115 g) day-old Poilâne-Style Sourdough (page 50) or other sourdough, tough crusts removed, cut into 1-inch (2.5-cm) pieces (about 2 cups)

10 large dried dates, pitted and coarsely chopped (if making the Fruit Compote variation on page 226, use only 5 dates)

6 tablespoons (90 ml) water

¼ cup (30 g) chopped walnuts

**FOR THE GANACHE**

9 ounces (255 g) bittersweet chocolate, finely chopped (about 1½ cups)

3 ounces (85 g) milk chocolate, finely chopped (about ½ cup)

1 cup (240 ml) heavy cream

4 tablespoons (2 ounces; 57 g) unsalted butter, cut into small pieces

Fine sea salt

Whipped cream and/or sliced seasonal fruit, for serving (optional)

**MAKE THE CRUST:** Put the bread, dates, walnuts, and water in a blender and let soak for 20 minutes. Blend until a "dough" forms.

Using your hands, press the date-walnut dough evenly into the bottom and up the sides of a 9-inch (23-cm) tart pan with a removable bottom. Cover and refrigerate for at least 8 hours, and up to 24 hours.

**WHEN READY TO ASSEMBLE THE TART, MAKE THE GANACHE:** In a medium bowl, combine the bittersweet and milk chocolates. In a small saucepan, combine the cream, butter, and a pinch of salt and heat over medium heat until the butter melts. Remove the pan from the heat and pour the hot liquid over the chocolate. Let sit for 1 minute, then stir until the chocolate is completely melted and smooth.

Pour the ganache into the chilled shell and refrigerate until set, at least 6 hours, and up to 24 hours; once the filling has set, cover the tart loosely with plastic wrap.

Slice the tart and serve cold, topped with sliced seasonal fruit and/or whipped cream, if you like.

continued

## Variation

### TRIPLE APPLE COMPOTE TART

For this autumnal filling, apples are cooked into a spiced apple compote, topped with sautéed apples, and garnished with diced raw apples for a hint of crunch. This is also delicious made with pears.

| | |
|---|---|
| Walnut-Date Bread Crust (page 224) | ¾ teaspoon apple cider vinegar |
| 7 medium cooking apples (1,350 g) | ½ teaspoon (0.25 g) ground cinnamon |
| 1½ tablespoons (30 ml) fresh lemon juice, plus a little more for sprinkling the apple slice | 2 pinches allspice |
| | 2 to 4 tablespoons water, if needed |
| 1 whole star anise | 2 tablespoons unsalted butter, plus more if needed |
| ¼ teaspoon (2 g) fine sea salt | |
| ⅓ cup (66 g) plus 1 teaspoon granulated sugar | ½ teaspoon fresh thyme leaves |
| | Unsweetened whipped cream or crème fraîche, for serving (optional) |
| ¼ cup (53 g) packed dark brown sugar | |

Press the date-walnut mixture evenly into the bottom and up the sides of the tart pan. Refrigerate.

Peel, core, and coarsely chop 4 of the apples. Combine the chopped apples, lemon juice, star anise, and salt in a large heavy pot, such as a Dutch oven. Set over medium heat, partially cover, and cook, stirring occasionally, until the apples release their juices and begin to soften, about 15 minutes.

Add the ⅓ cup (66 g) granulated sugar, the brown sugar, vinegar, cinnamon, and a pinch of allspice. Partially cover again and cook, stirring and occasionally scraping the bottom of the pot, until the apples caramelize to a dark brown and break down and the mixture thickens, about 30 minutes; add the water as needed if the pot looks dry. Remove and discard the star anise and mash any large pieces of apple to make a uniform puree. Let cool to room temperature. (The apple compote will keep, covered and refrigerated, for up to 2 weeks.)

Spoon the apple compote into the tart shell and refrigerate until chilled. Shortly before serving, core the remaining 3 apples and cut each into 12 wedges. Sprinkle 1 wedge with a bit of lemon juice and set aside.

Heat the butter in a large skillet. Add half of the apple wedges. Sprinkle with ½ teaspoon of the granulated sugar and cook, turning the apples occasionally, until they are tender and nicely browned, 5 to 10 minutes. Transfer to a plate. Add the remaining apple wedges (except for the reserved wedge) to the skillet, sprinkle with the remaining granulated sugar, and cook until tender and browned, adding more butter if needed. Transfer to the plate and let cool to room temperature.

Arrange the sautéed apples, overlapping them slightly, in a ring around the perimeter of the tart. Peel the reserved apple wedge and finely dice. Pile the diced apple in the center of the tart and sprinkle with the remaining pinch of allspice. Sprinkle the tart with thyme leaves and serve with whipped cream or crème fraîche, if desired.

# Walnut Financiers

Financiers are small, very moist cakes made with ground nuts and fragrant brown butter. Here I substitute bread crumbs from our Walnut Sourdough for the usual ground nuts to yield a lighter cake. Be sure to use very stale bread so the crumbs don't add too much extra moisture.

MAKES TWELVE 4-BY-2-INCH (10-BY-5-CM) FINANCIERS OR 12 CUPCAKE-SIZE CAKES

| | |
|---|---|
| 8 tablespoons (4 ounces; 113 g) unsalted butter, plus more for the pan | 4 large egg whites |
| | Fine sea salt |
| 2 tablespoons (30 ml) honey | 2½ cups (200 g) dried bread crumbs (see page 181) from Walnut Sourdough (page 52) or other nut bread (see note) |
| ½ cup (60 g) confectioners' sugar | |

Position a rack in the middle and preheat the oven to 375°F (190°C). Generously butter twelve 4-by-2-inch (10-by-5-cm) financier molds or regular-size cupcake molds.

In a medium saucepan, cook the butter over medium heat, stirring often, until it foams, then browns and becomes very fragrant, 5 to 8 minutes. Transfer to a large bowl and whisk in the honey. Let cool completely.

Whisk the confectioners' sugar, egg whites, and a pinch of salt into the butter mixture until combined. Fold in the bread crumbs and nuts, if using.

Spoon the mixture evenly into the molds and bake until golden and set, 14 to 18 minutes. Transfer the pan(s) to a wire rack and let cool completely before unmolding.

Store the financiers, covered, at room temperature for up to 3 days, or wrap well in plastic wrap and freeze for up to 3 months.

---

NOTE: You can also use 2¼ cups (156 g) crumbs from Poilâne-Style Sourdough (page 50) plus ¼ cup (40 g) finely ground walnuts for the bread crumbs.

# Saffron and Lemon Baba au Rhum

Brioche, besides making a lovely breakfast toast, is sweet enough to work as an ingredient in dessert. Here a loaf of it replaces the traditional yeasted sponge cake for baba au rhum. The brioche should be stale so it can soak up the syrup flavored with lemon, rum, and saffron. The saffron, which adds an intriguing flavor, was often included in recipes for the dessert in the mid-1800s. For best results, used aged rum agricole. Made of cane sugar instead of molasses, it is aromatic and less sweet than regular dark rum.

**SERVES 8 TO 10**

1¼ cups (250 g) sugar

Zest of ½ lemon, removed in strips with a vegetable peeler

Large pinch saffron

2 cups (480 ml) water

½ cup (120 ml) dark rum, preferably rum agricole

One 2- to 3-day-old loaf Brioche (page 91) or other brioche

Whipped cream, for serving

Sliced fresh peaches or other juicy fruit, such as pears or pineapple, for serving (optional)

Combine the sugar, lemon zest, saffron, and water in a small saucepan and cook over medium-high heat, stirring, until the sugar dissolves. Remove the pan from the heat and let cool completely. Remove and discard the lemon zest. Add ¼ cup (60 ml) of the rum.

Place the brioche on its side in a casserole dish or deep baking pan large enough to hold it comfortably. Slowly pour over half of the syrup and allow the brioche to soak up as much of it as possible. Turn the brioche and pour over the remaining syrup. Cover with plastic wrap and refrigerate for at least 6 hours, and up to 24 hours, turning the brioche in the syrup occasionally.

To serve, put the brioche right side up on a rimmed platter. Place the remaining ¼ cup (60 ml) rum in a small skillet and use a long-handled match to carefully ignite it, averting your face. When the flames are extinguished, pour the mixture over the brioche. Slice the brioche and serve, topped with whipped cream and fruit, if you like.

# Toasted-Bread Mendiant Ice Cream

*Mendiants* (MON-dee-yon), chocolate disks topped with nuts and dried fruit, are a classic Christmastime treat. The base for this ice cream, flavored with cubes of our Walnut Sourdough and Rye Loaf with Currants, recalls their flavor but has deep toasty undertones. The trick is to toast the bread slices until they are very dark to remove as much moisture as possible before cutting them into cubes.

MAKES 1 QUART (950 G)

2 ounces (57 g; about a 1-inch/2.5-cm slice) Walnut Sourdough (page 52) or other nut bread

2 ounces (57 g; about a 1-inch/2.5-cm slice) Rye Loaf with Currants (page 60) or raisin bread

2½ cups (600 ml) whole milk

1¼ cups (300 ml) heavy cream

¼ teaspoon (2 g) fine sea salt

4 large egg yolks

⅓ cup (80 g) sugar

Toast the bread slices on both sides until dark brown. Cut into 1-inch (2.5-cm) pieces.

In a medium saucepan, combine the bread cubes, milk, cream, and salt and bring almost to a boil over medium-high heat. Remove the pan from the heat, cover, and set aside for at least 1 hour, and up to overnight, in the refrigerator.

Strain the cream mixture through a fine-mesh sieve into a medium bowl, using the back of a spoon to press the bread against the sieve to extract as much liquid as possible. Discard the bread.

Fill a large bowl with ice water and set a medium heatproof bowl inside it. In another large bowl, with a whisk or hand mixer, whisk together the egg yolks and sugar until the mixture lightens in color and increases in volume. Whisk in the cream mixture, then pour into a large heavy-bottomed saucepan. Set the pan over medium heat and cook, stirring constantly with a wooden spoon, until the mixture thickens, 5 to 8 minutes; do not let the mixture boil.

Remove the pan from the heat and strain the custard through a fine-mesh sieve into the bowl set in the ice water. Let cool to room temperature, stirring frequently. Remove the bowl from the ice water and place a piece of plastic wrap directly on the custard's surface. Refrigerate until cold.

Transfer the chilled custard to an ice cream maker and churn according to the manufacturer's instructions. Transfer to a freezer container and freeze until ready to serve.

# Beer Granita with Brioche

Imagine my delight when I learned that bread and ice cream is a classic breakfast in Sicily. The Sicilians pair a refreshing icy granita (*granité* in French) with a brioche roll. Although this version, made with beer, may be better suited for the evening, I won't judge if you eat some first thing in the morning. Use whichever beer you enjoy drinking, but remember that the more bitter the beer, the more bitter the granita. To eat the dish like an Italian, pull off bits of brioche and dunk into the granita as it melts.

SERVES 6 TO 8

3 cups (720 ml) beer

¾ cup (180 ml) water

⅓ cup packed (56 g) light brown sugar

Pinch of fine sea salt

2 teaspoons (4 g) finely grated lemon zest, or more to taste

Pinch of flaky sea salt

Whipped cream or Brioche Whipped Cream (opposite), for serving (optional)

6 to 8 slices Brioche (page 91) or other brioche

In a medium bowl, whisk together the beer, water, brown sugar, and salt until the sugar and salt dissolve. Pour the mixture into a shallow 9-by-13-inch (23-by-33-cm) baking pan (preferably metal) and place in the freezer until the mixture begins to freeze around the edges, 2 to 3 hours.

Use a fork to stir the mixture, breaking up any large pieces of ice and raking the shards and crystals toward the center. Return the pan to the freezer and continue to scrape the mixture with a fork every 30 minutes until you have very fine crystals. Cover and keep frozen until ready to serve. *(The granita will keep, covered tightly, for 1 month.)*

Scrape the granita with a fork into bowls and serve topped with the zest, flaky salt, and whipped cream, if you like, with the brioche on the side.

# Brioche Whipped Cream

Infusing cream with brioche gives it buttery, toasty accents. Serve with Apple Tarts (page 204), fruit crumbles, or other fruit desserts.

**MAKES ABOUT 2 CUPS (475 ML)**

1 cup (240 ml) heavy cream

2 thick slices day-old Brioche (page 91) or other brioche, torn into 1-inch (2.5-cm) pieces

Put the cream and brioche in a medium saucepan and bring just to a boil over medium-high heat, stirring occasionally. Remove the pan from the heat, cover with a tight-fitting lid, and let cool. Let stand at room temperature for at least 2 hours, or up to overnight in the refrigerator.

Strain the cream through a fine-mesh sieve into a large bowl, using the back of a spoon to press the brioche against the strainer to extract as much liquid as possible. Discard the bread and refrigerate the cream, if necessary, until well chilled, about 1 hour.

With a whisk or a hand mixer on medium speed, beat the cream until soft peaks form. Use immediately, or cover and refrigerate for up to 4 hours.

# Chocolate-Covered Bread Chips

These confections of toasty bread crisps bathed in dark chocolate are reminiscent of chocolate-covered pretzels and make a perfect snack or post-dinner bite. They take just moments to whip up.

MAKES ABOUT 16 PIECES

4 ounces (113 g) Bread Chips (page 182), broken into ½-inch (1.25-cm) pieces (about 2 cups)

8 ounces (226 g) dark chocolate, coarsely chopped

Ground spice of your choice; I like cardamom (optional)

Line a plate or platter with parchment paper. Put the bread chip pieces in a medium bowl.

In a medium microwavable bowl, melt the chocolate in the microwave (or melt it in a double boiler). Pour the melted chocolate over the bread chips, sprinkle with a pinch of spice, if using, and stir with a silicone spatula or wooden spoon until the chips are coated.

Using a spoon, scoop up clusters of chocolate-coated bread chips and transfer to the prepared plate. Let set at cool room temperature or refrigerate to harden. Store, covered, at room temperature for up to 4 days.

# Part Three

# Nighttime

# DREAMS and EXPLORATIONS

# Dreams and Explorations

I'VE ALWAYS LOVED MIDNIGHT. Because France follows a twenty-four-hour clock, a digital clock at that hour displays four zeros, which, to me, look like two infinity signs. So the hour suggests not only a new day, but also unlimited possibilities ahead.

It's often around this time, after a long and busy day, that I can reflect on not only what has been but on what is yet to come. It's also when our night shift begins. Some of my very first stints in the bakery were on this shift. The notion was exciting at first: the quiet, knowing you were doing something productive while others slept, and focusing on the task at hand with a single-mindedness not easily found during the distractions of the day.

But the night shift is also hard, tiring, and lonely. After a few hours, the mind wanders. Back when I was sixteen, my thoughts might stray to my friends. Were they out having fun while I was in a basement mixing flour and water? I also wondered why I had to spend time alone in the bakehouse when my own father despised the solitude and lack of connectedness. But then the bread would beckon, and such thoughts would dissolve like the salt in the water for our starter.

These days, when I bake at night, my thoughts center on my dreams for the future of Poilâne. Ever since my parents passed away, people have been asking me, "What will be the Apollonia touch?" At first the question annoyed me; taking over the business was not about my own ego, it was about what Poilâne would bring to the world. My grandfather offered something unique: a dark, giant country loaf during the times of pale, prissy baguettes. Then my father, looking for a way to transcend the bakery's physical walls, not only expanded the business but also expanded on bread's place in art and politics and society.

Straddling tradition and modernity, I very slowly started to put my mark on the business. Among my first creations were the whimsical spoon-shaped *sablés* (shortbread-like cookies) we serve with coffee at Comptoir Poilâne; customers are encouraged to use them as a stirrer and then eat them. (We also sell them packaged at the bakery.) As I experimented with flavoring them differently, crafting varieties from ingredients found in other cuisines (such as dried yuzu) or inspired by someone specific (violet and licorice for two children from the neighborhood), I also began exploring different grains. In the process, I discovered that is was what I like to do most.

Throughout my life, bread has been a way to explore different cultures. When I travel, physically or through books, I make connections with the bread traditions of other countries. Because of this, one of my parents' friends calls me "Bread Trotter," a nickname that describes my insatiable appetite for bread, its culture, and its spirit.

When I first traveled to Japan, for instance, I saw how the bowl of rice that accompanies a meal plays the same role as the bread and butter served along with a meal in France. The same is true of a baked potato in Ireland, or of injera, the spongy, stretchy flatbread that doubles as a serving utensil in Ethiopia. In the wee hours of the night, I ponder all these iterations and contemplate how they can influence Poilâne's direction.

Looking toward the future, my team and I have been experimenting in baking. Our approach is uncompromising. We always use a single type of grain flour for bread in order to showcase its singular flavor. This is in line with our tradition: Unlike the way many bakers in the United States combine different types of flour in their breads, bakers in France tend to make bread using a single grain.

These days I'm taking bigger, bolder steps and breaking down boundaries as I contemplate the question "Just what *is* bread?" In France, the answer has long been simple: Bread is made of wheat flour (or, less commonly, rye), water, and a leavening agent. But over the years, I've broadened that definition. Now when formulating my answer, I consider the traditions of other countries, experiment with grains other than wheat and rye, and research fermentation beyond bread baking.

In 2006 I decided that rethinking corn-based bread, a treat I fell in love with while at Harvard, would be our first foray into the future. Most recipes are made with a combination of flour and cornmeal and, more often than not, plenty of sugar and eggs. I worked with our master baker to craft a bread from 100 percent corn flour (very fine cornmeal). Little did I know that it would take us ten years to fashion a loaf we felt confident presenting to our customers. Finding the right substitute for the gluten normally provided by wheat flour proved challenging, and we also wanted to make the recipe vegan and sugar-free.

In batch after batch, we experimented with various options to stand in for the wheat flour, sugar, and dairy products. In the end, flax seeds and oat milk were the keys. Finally, Poilâne's corn bread was born!

Our research and development extend beyond bread. Since my early tests of corn bread, I've been focusing on the other grains highlighted in this chapter in order to explore what they have to offer beyond their traditional uses. Take oats, for example. I grew up eating oatmeal as part of a hearty winter breakfast, thanks to my American mother's love of it. My own attachment to it prompted me to toy with making oat milk. (Well, that and my guilt after realizing I had let a barely touched bottle of cow's milk spoil. I switched to oat milk, which I could make as needed, as my standard house milk.) I began testing it in cooking and baking. I use oat milk in sweets and treats featured at Comptoir Poilâne, where customers can also add oat milk to their coffee if they like. Indeed, many of our non-bread explorations, including our grain salads, have become popular menu items, making the café in essence a working lab.

Drinks are another side of fermentation: Grains have been used to produce alcohol for millennia. In fact, my father used to affectionately call one of his oldest friends in the beer business "Liquid Bread" because of the similarities between the products they sold.

I never gave the nickname my father bestowed on his friend much thought as child, but I've come to understand that the endearment was all about making connections and reflected my father's ability to build bridges between worlds. For my father, bread was much more than something to eat. It was, like those double zeros on the digital clock, connecting to yesterday and tomorrow.

As third-generation Poilânes, my sister and I are, of course, rooted in our family's traditions. As this book was being written, my sister had a baby, which means there's another generation who may one day take over the business. My hope is that when this happens, Poilâne will have moved seamlessly into the future while continuing to embrace its past, something achieved by my grandfather, my father, and now by me.

A cornfield in the Basque Country near the Pyrenees, where Poilâne's corn is grown

# Sweet Corn Brioche

In France, corn is largely viewed as an imported water-thirsty crop that regularly makes the headlines in connection with GMOs. I love it anyway. It wasn't until I went to college that I discovered the pure pleasure of American cornbread. At Harvard, individual cornbread loaves were served with the Sunday meal. They were sweet and scone-like, so much so that I often ate a second one topped with a bit of butter as my dessert.

This buttery cornmeal brioche calls to mind that treat. Orange blossom water brightens its flavor, but you can omit it for a more traditional result.

MAKES TWO 9-BY-5-INCH (23-BY-13-CM) LOAVES

| | |
|---|---|
| 5 large eggs, at room temperature | 1 package (2¼ teaspoons; 7 g) active dry yeast |
| ⅓ cup packed (56 g) light brown sugar | 2 teaspoons (11 g) fine sea salt |
| 1 tablespoon (15 ml) orange blossom water (optional) | 2¼ sticks (9 ounces; 255 g) unsalted butter, cubed and softened until just pliable, plus more for the bowls and pans |
| 260 g (2 cups) all-purpose flour | |
| 240 g (2 cups) corn flour (very finely ground cornmeal) | 1 large egg, beaten with 1 tablespoon (15 ml) water for egg wash |

In the bowl of a stand mixer fitted with the paddle attachment, beat together the eggs, brown sugar, and orange blossom water on medium-low speed until the sugar dissolves, 2 to 3 minutes. Add both flours, the yeast, and salt and mix until combined. Switch to the dough hook and, with the mixer on medium speed, add the butter 1 tablespoon at a time, waiting until each addition is almost completely mixed in before adding the next, then continue mixing until all the butter is fully incorporated and the dough is elastic and sticky,

10 to 15 minutes. You should be able to pull on the dough without it immediately breaking.

Butter two large bowls. Divide the dough in half, shape each piece into a ball, and transfer to the bowls. Cover with plastic wrap or kitchen towels and set aside in a warm (72°F to 77°F/22°C to 25°C), draft-free place until almost doubled in size, 1 hour to 1 hour 15 minutes.

Generously butter two 9-by-5-inch (23-by-13-cm) loaf pans. Gently transfer one piece of risen dough to a clean work surface. Gently stretch the two opposite sides of the dough and fold over into the center, then repeat with the top and bottom to form a round; be careful not to tear or deflate the dough too much. Gently roll it into a 9-inch (23-cm)-long log and nestle it, seam side down, in one of the pans. Repeat with the second piece of dough. Cover loosely with plastic wrap and set aside to proof in a warm, draft-free place until the dough rises to the tops of the pans, 1½ to 2 hours.

Position a rack in the lower third and preheat the oven to 350°F (180°C).

*continued*

Using a pastry brush, brush each loaf with the egg wash and then, using a pair of scissors, snip each top 5 or 6 times lengthwise down the middle. Let rest for 5 minutes, then place the pans in the oven and bake until golden, 45 minutes to 1 hour 30 minutes. Check the loaves after 30 to 40 minutes and cover loosely with aluminum foil if the tops are browning too quickly.

When the loaves are done, immediately remove them from the pans and let cool completely on a wire rack before slicing.

Stored in paper bags or wrapped in linen at room temperature, the brioche will keep for 3 to 5 days. For longer storage, wrap well in plastic wrap and freeze for up to 3 months.

# Chicha Morada

This Peruvian drink is typically made with purple corn, pineapple (for acidity), and cinnamon, but I switched that up when creating my version. I wanted to use ingredients native to Peru, but they're hard to come by in France. Since it's difficult to find purple corn, I use standard yellow corn and add cocoa powder—which is a Peruvian ingredient—for color and flavor. Chicha morada is delicious served warm like mulled wine, or chilled and poured over ice. Feel free to top a cold one with a little cold beer. I also like this sweetened with a cup of pineapple juice.

MAKES ABOUT 4 CUPS (960 ML); SERVES 4

2 quarts (1.9 liter) water

2 ears corn, shucked

2 tablespoons (15 g) unsweetened cocoa powder

½ medium red chile (seeds removed and discarded if you want less heat)

In a large saucepan, combine the water, corn, cocoa powder, and chile and bring to a boil over high heat, then reduce the heat to low and simmer until the liquid is reduced by half, about 2 hours. Remove and discard the corn and chile.

Serve hot or cold.

# Corn-Flour Bread

Gluten-free, vegan, and delicious, my corn-flour bread is the result of many years of trial and error. The rich, full flavor of corn shines through, unencumbered by the dairy, sugar, and eggs found in most traditional recipes. This loaf is entirely different from the cake-like cornbread favored in the U.S. Its air pockets resemble the crumb of a sourdough and keep the loaf light, while flecks of flax seed, which act as the emulsifier in place of eggs, add texture.

It's important to use corn flour, cornmeal so finely ground that its texture resembles all-purpose flour; if you use coarser cornmeal, the bread's texture will be grainy.

MAKES ONE 9-BY-5-INCH (23-BY-13-CM) LOAF

3 tablespoons (32 g) flax seeds

1⅔ cups (400 ml) oat milk, homemade (page 261) or store-bought

Vegetable oil, for the pan

240 g (2 cups) corn flour (very finely ground cornmeal)

Scant 1 tablespoon (9 g) active dry yeast

1 teaspoon (6 g) fine sea salt

1 cup (150 g) skinned hazelnuts, toasted and crushed coarsely (optional)

Using a mortar and pestle or a rolling pin, coarsely crush the flax seeds. In a small bowl, soak the seeds in ⅔ cup (160 ml) of the oat milk for 1 hour at room temperature, or cover and refrigerate for up to 24 hours.

Lightly oil a 9-by-5-inch (23-by-13-cm) loaf pan.

In a large bowl, combine the corn flour, yeast, and salt. Pour the oat milk mixture over the dry ingredients, then add the remaining 1 cup (240 ml) oat milk and the hazelnuts, if using, and thoroughly combine with a wooden spoon.

Scrape the batter into the prepared loaf pan and let rise in a warm (72°F to 77°F/22°C to 25°C), draft-free place for an hour, or until slightly risen.

Position a rack in the lower third and preheat the oven to 400°F (200°C).

Bake the bread until it just starts to brown on the edges, about 1 hour. Transfer to a wire rack and let cool completely before slicing. Stored in a paper bag or wrapped in linen at room temperature, the loaf will keep for up to 3 days.

# Rice "Bread"

When I started to think about the similarities between rice and bread, and how in Japan rice is served with every meal as bread is in France, I imagined a combination of the two: a "slice" of rice that could be held in the hand like a slice of bread and eaten alongside all the things bread typically accompanies, from stews to a juicy roast chicken.

The key to having the slices stay intact is to not rinse the rice before cooking it. This, plus the inherent stickiness of sushi rice, binds the "bread." While I have used a round cake pan in the recipe below, you can use a loaf pan to make sandwich-style slices if you like.

MAKES ONE 8-INCH (20-CM) ROUND "LOAF";
SERVES 6 TO 8

1 cup (185 g) sushi rice
(do not rinse)

1 cup (185 g) jasmine rice
or other long-grain white
rice (do not rinse)

3 tablespoons (45 ml)
rice wine vinegar

1 tablespoon (15 ml) mirin

1 tablespoon (13 g) sugar

2 tablespoons (18 g)
sesame seeds, toasted

Cook the sushi rice according to the package directions until al dente. Cook the jasmine rice according to the package directions until just tender but with a bit of resistance.

Meanwhile, in a small saucepan, whisk together the rice wine vinegar, mirin, and sugar and warm over medium-low heat just until the sugar dissolves. Remove from the heat and let cool.

In a large bowl, mix together the warm cooked rices. Pour the rice wine mixture over the rice and use a wooden spoon to mix gently.

Line an 8-inch (20-cm) round cake pan with plastic wrap. Spoon the seasoned rice mixture into the prepared pan, pressing it in the pan to compact it, and sprinkle with the sesame seeds. Refrigerate until chilled and set, at least 2 hours, and up to overnight.

Slice the rice bread into wedges and serve cold or at room temperature.

# Corn, Rice, and Barley Sablés

A sablé (sah-BLAY), a cookie whose name translates as "sandy," has a crumbly, melt-in-your-mouth texture, making it perfect with a cup of tea or an espresso. The three different doughs that follow are made with just a few ingredients and allow the flavor of the grain to come forward. The method is the same for each, though the proportions of the other ingredients vary because of the differences in the respective flours.

### CORN SABLÉS

MAKES 60 TO 70 COOKIES

½ cup plus 1 tablespoon (125 g) sugar

1 large egg plus 1 large egg yolk, at room temperature

2¼ sticks (9 ounces; 250 g) unsalted butter, cut into cubes, softened

240 g (2 cups) corn flour (very finely ground cornmeal)

240 g (2 cups) all-purpose flour, plus more for rolling

### RICE SABLÉS

MAKES 60 TO 70 COOKIES

¾ cup plus 1 tablespoon (175 g) sugar

1 large egg plus 1 large egg yolk, at room temperature

2¼ sticks (9 ounces; 250 g) unsalted butter, cut into cubes, softened

500 g (3¼ cups) brown rice flour, plus more for rolling

### BARLEY SABLÉS

MAKES 20 TO 25 COOKIES

¼ cup (85 g) sugar

1 large egg, at room temperature

9 tablespoons (4½ ounces; 125 g) unsalted butter, cut into cubes, softened

240 g (2 cups) barley flour, plus more for rolling

In a large bowl, with a handheld mixer on medium speed, whisk the sugar and egg (or egg and egg yolk) until frothy, about 2 minutes. Add the butter and mix until combined, 1 to 2 minutes. Add the flour(s) and mix until just incorporated; do not overmix.

Lightly flour a work surface and turn the dough out onto it. Divide the corn or rice dough in half and shape into 2 disks; shape the barley dough into 1 disk. Wrap in plastic wrap and refrigerate for 30 minutes. (*The dough can be frozen for up to 3 months; thaw for at least 3 hours at room temperature before rolling.*)

Line two baking sheets with parchment paper.

Lightly flour a work surface and a rolling pin. Roll the dough out ¼ inch (0.6 cm) thick, reflouring the surface and pin as needed. Cut out 2-inch (5-cm) rounds and place ½ inch (1.25 cm) apart on the baking sheets. Gather the scraps, reroll, and cut out more cookies. Refrigerate the cookies on the baking sheets for 30 minutes before baking.

Position racks in the upper and lower thirds and preheat the oven to 350°F (180°C).

Bake the cookies until the centers are set, 13 to 15 minutes. Rotate the pans from top to bottom and front to back halfway through the baking time. Immediately transfer the cookies to a wire rack and let cool completely.

Store the cookies in an airtight container for up to a week.

---

NOTE: None of the sablé recipes includes salt; for more savory cookies that would be at home on a cheese plate, use salted butter.

# Oat Milk

It wasn't until a run-in with soy milk in college that I took a close look at plant-based milk alternatives. Soy milk lacks the freshness of cow's milk. Almond milk, while closest in texture to cow's milk, is a problem for people who are allergic to tree nuts. Rice and hazelnut milk are too sweet for my taste, while hemp and spelt milk are grainy. Oat milk, which is becoming more available in stores, has a lovely freshness, plus a creamy texture, and is not too sweet. It's a cost-efeective alternative to cow's milk, especially for coffee. While you can buy it, many commercial versions contain lots of sugar, and it's really easy to make at home.

MAKES ABOUT 4 CUPS (950 ML)

4¼ cups (1 liter) water

Fine sea salt

1½ cups (150 g) old-fashioned rolled oats

In a blender, combine the water, oats, and a pinch of salt. Blend until combined and set aside to rest for 30 minutes.

Set a fine-mesh sieve over a bowl and strain the milk, pressing on the solids to release as much liquid as possible. (Discard the oats or use in a smoothie.) Use immediately, or refrigerate in an airtight container for up to 3 days. Shake well before using.

# Oat-Milk Rice Pudding

In France, we love our *riz au lait* ("rice pudding"). It's not only made at home and in restaurants but is also found in most supermarkets, usually in plastic or glass jars that resemble yogurt containers. With its creamy texture, it's one of our favorite comfort foods. Oat milk has a natural sweetness, so you only need to add a small amount of sugar and, because oat milk thickens when you heat it, the pudding thickens nicely.

**SERVES 4**

3 cups (720 ml) oat milk, homemade (page 261) or store-bought

¾ cup (150 g) Arborio rice

¼ cup (45 g) turbinado sugar

½ vanilla bean, split, seeds scraped out, seeds and pod reserved

1 bay leaf

Fine sea salt

1 cup (about 150 g) chopped toasted nuts, such as almonds, pistachios, pecans, or walnuts (optional)

In a large saucepan, combine the oat milk, rice, sugar, vanilla seeds and pod, bay leaf, and a pinch of salt and bring to a boil over high heat. Reduce the heat to low and cook, stirring occasionally with a wooden spoon or silicone spatula so the bottom doesn't burn, until the rice is tender and the liquid has mostly been absorbed, 25 to 30 minutes.

Remove the bay leaf and vanilla pod and serve warm, topped with the chopped nuts, if you like, or chill to serve cold. The pudding will keep, covered and refrigerated, for up to 3 days.

# Chocolate, Pear, and Oat-Cream Charlotte

A charlotte is a beloved French dessert made by lining a mold with ladyfingers and filling the center with a mousse, custard, whipped cream, or fruit, or a combination of all of those. The charlotte is unmolded to serve, and for a dessert that's so easy to make, it looks striking. In this recipe, a mousse made with oat milk to offset the richness of the chocolate is paired with pears. I use spice cake in place of the usual ladyfingers.

To make a thick, creamy oat milk, the oats must be soaked in the water for up to 24 hours, so plan ahead.

SERVES 6 TO 8

**FOR THE CHOCOLATE OAT CREAM**

1 cup (100 g) old-fashioned rolled oats

3 cups (720 ml) water

Fine sea salt

3¼ ounces (100 g) bittersweet chocolate, coarsely chopped (about ¾ cup)

**FOR THE CHARLOTTE**

3 ripe pears, peeled, cored, and chopped into ½-inch (1.25-cm) pieces

1 tablespoon (15 ml) fresh lemon juice

2 tablespoons (10 g) unsweetened cocoa powder

1 Spice Cake (page 219) or 1½ pounds (650 g) store-bought spice cake or gingerbread

⅓ cup (50 g) maple crunchies or ⅓ cup (27 g) maple sprinkles (see Sources, page 277), or ⅓ cup (43 g) cocoa nibs (optional)

Chocolate shavings, for garnish (optional)

**MAKE THE CHOCOLATE OAT CREAM:** Put the oats in a medium bowl and cover with water by 1 inch (2.5 cm). Let soak, refrigerated, for at least 8 hours, and up to 24 hours.

Drain the oats in a fine-mesh sieve; discard the water. Transfer the oats to a blender, add the 3 cups (720 ml) water and a pinch of salt, and blend until very smooth. Set aside for 1 hour.

Strain the oat milk through a fine-mesh sieve set over a bowl; discard the oats or use in a smoothie. *(The oat milk can be refrigerated in an airtight container for up to 3 days.)*

Transfer the oat milk to a saucepan and bring to a boil over medium-high heat, whisking often. Add the chocolate, reduce the heat to low, and simmer, stirring, until the chocolate melts and the mixture thickens to a custard-like texture, 3 to 5 minutes. Transfer to a bowl and let cool.

**ASSEMBLE THE CHARLOTTE:** In a large bowl, toss the pears with the lemon juice and cocoa powder. Set aside.

Line a charlotte mold or an 8-inch (20-cm) springform pan with plastic wrap so that a few inches hang over the sides.

Cut the spice cake into ½-inch (1.25-cm)-thick slices, then trim the slices to the same height as the mold or pan; save the scraps to line the bottom of the pan. Line the sides of the pan with the slices, placing them snugly side by side so there are no gaps. Line the bottom with the remaining slices and scraps, cutting them as necessary to fit snugly.

Fold the pear mixture and the crunchies, sprinkles, or nibs, if using, into the cooled chocolate oat cream, then spoon into the mold. Fold the edges of the plastic wrap over the charlotte to prevent a skin from forming; add another sheet of plastic if needed to cover the top completely. Refrigerate the charlotte until chilled, at least 5 hours, and up to 24 hours.

To unmold the charlotte, remove the extra sheet of plastic if you used it. Gently pull up on the edges of the plastic wrap to lift it out of the mold, or release and remove the outer ring of the springform pan and lift it away. Use an offset spatula or other large spatula to transfer the charlotte to a platter or cake stand. Serve cold, sprinkled with chocolate shavings, if you like.

# Caramelized Peach and Barley Crumble

This recipe was inspired by an idea that came to me while I was visiting the Masumoto peach farm in California. I was sad to see how many peaches were rejected for the tiniest imperfection, but it gave me solace to learn that they were used to infuse locally brewed beer with their superior flavor. Here, a crumble topping made from rolled barley (the flakes are similar to oatmeal, which you can substitute) underscores the nutty barley notes in the beer.

SERVES 6 TO 9

3 tablespoons (1½ ounces; 42 g) salted butter

9 medium peaches (2¾ pounds; 1.25 kg), pitted and quartered, or a mix of peaches and strawberries or raspberries

1 cup (240 ml) beer, such as brown ale

2 cups (200 g) rolled barley or old-fashioned rolled oats

6 tablespoons (3 ounces; 84 g) unsalted butter, cubed and very cold

1½ tablespoons (21 ml) honey

Ice cream, for serving (optional)

Position a rack in the middle and preheat the oven to 375°F (190°C).

In a large deep skillet, melt half of the salted butter over medium heat. Add half the peaches and cook, tossing occasionally, until browned and fragrant, about 5 minutes. Transfer to a bowl and repeat with the remaining salted butter and peaches.

Return all the peaches to the pan, pour in the beer, and simmer until the beer has almost evaporated, 10 to 15 minutes. Transfer the peaches to a 9-inch (23-cm) square baking dish.

In a large bowl, combine the rolled barley or oats, unsalted butter, and honey. Use your hands to press and pinch the ingredients together to form a crumble. Sprinkle the crumble evenly over the peaches.

Bake until golden brown, 20 to 25 minutes. Let cool slightly on a wire rack.

Serve the crumble warm, topped with ice cream, if you like. Leftover crumble will keep, covered and refrigerated, for 2 days. Serve cold or at room temperature, or gently reheat in a low oven.

# Homemade Orgeat Syrup

Barley was one of the first cultivated grains, and as such it has played an important role in beverages around the world. Fermented, it's used to make barley wine and, of course, beer. The grains are roasted to make a tea that's a staple in much of Asia.

Barley was originally a main ingredient in orgeat, an almond syrup used in cocktails. In fact, the French word for barley is *orge*, from the Latin *hordeaceus*, "made with barley."

When I was growing up, one of my favorite drinks was water flavored with the syrup. Nowadays, the recipe for orgeat has morphed into an almond-only syrup. My homemade version, though, is made with barley and almonds, and it includes a little orange blossom water, which is also traditional. The result is a fresh-tasting version of the commercial syrup. Use it in the aperitif on page 270, or in place of store-bought orgeat syrup in a Mai Tai, or add some to Champagne for a delicious alternative to a Kir Royale. It's also a refreshing flavoring for seltzer water. Plan ahead; the barley and almonds need to soak overnight.

MAKES 2 CUPS (480 ML)

¼ cup (50 g) pearled barley

¼ cup (30 g) coarsely chopped raw almonds

1¼ cups (300 ml) water

2 cups (425 g) sugar

Few drops orange blossom water

In a medium bowl, combine the barley, almonds, and water. Cover with plastic wrap and refrigerate overnight.

Strain the barley mixture through a fine-mesh sieve into a medium saucepan, pressing on the solids with the back of a wooden spoon to extract as much liquid as possible. Discard the solids. Add the sugar, bring to a simmer over medium heat, and simmer, stirring occasionally, until the sugar dissolves. Remove the pan from the heat and let cool completely.

Stir the orange blossom water into the cooled syrup. Transfer to an airtight container and chill before using. The orgeat will keep for at least a month in the refrigerator.

# La Mauresque

La Mauresque is a simple but delicious aperitif made by mixing pastis, orgeat, and ice water. The drink originally hails from the South of France, but it has become more popular in Paris with the explosion of the city's cocktail scene. Once considered a "lady's drink" because the sweet syrup lessens the intensity of the alcohol-forward anise-flavored liqueur, the refreshing drink is now enjoyed by men and women alike, especially during summer.

MAKES 1 APERITIF

2 ounces (60 ml) pastis

2 tablespoons (30 ml) Homemade Orgeat Syrup (page 268) or store-bought orgeat syrup

Chilled club soda or sparkling water, or ice water

Fresh mint sprig for garnish (optional)

Chill a highball or Collins glass. (To do this quickly, swirl some ice in the glass and then dump it out.) Add the pastis and orgeat syrup and stir to combine. Add ice, if desired, then fill the glass with club soda or ice water to taste (a 4:1 or 5:1 ratio is typical). Garnish with mint, if you like, and serve.

# Barley-Beer Bread

Once, when we were kids, my father brought me and my sister to an abandoned malt factory outside Antwerp, Belgium. He led us through a trapdoor into an old empty grain silo and told us to rub the wall with our fingers to bring out the barley aroma that had been trapped in the wall for decades. Sure enough we could smell, however faintly, the toasted cereal scent, and we marveled at how we could conjure up the past just like that. This deeply flavored, moist bread, made with beer and barley flour, is that memory manifested. Because barley flour alone can be overpoweringly sweet and produce a heavy texture, I have lightened the dough with the addition of wheat flour for a result that's reminiscent of pumpernickel bread.

MAKES ONE 9-BY-5-INCH (23-BY-13-CM) LOAF

250 g (1⅓ cups) of the starter from Poilâne-Style Sourdough (page 50)

240 g (1¾ cups) all-purpose flour

100 g (¾ cup plus 1 tablespoon) barley flour

1¼ teaspoons (7.5 g) fine sea salt

1 tablespoon (10 g) active dry yeast

1⅔ cups (400 ml) amber beer

Put the sourdough starter in the bowl of a stand mixer fitted with the whisk attachment. Add both flours, the salt, and yeast, add the beer, and mix with a wooden spoon to break up the starter and begin to combine the ingredients. Then whisk on medium speed for 10 minutes to aerate the dough. Let the dough rise in the bowl for 45 minutes; it will rise just slightly.

Mix the dough briefly again, then transfer to a 9-by-5-inch (23-by-13-cm) loaf pan. Let rise at room temperature until the dough reaches the top of the pan, about 2 hours.

Position a rack in the lower third and preheat the oven to 400°F (200°C).

Bake the bread until the edges are golden brown, about 1 hour 15 minutes. Transfer to a wire rack before slicing. Stored in a paper bag or wrapped in linen at room temperature, the bread will keep for 3 to 4 days.

NOTE: As with our sourdough, you will either need to have the starter on hand or plan ahead to make it, which takes a couple of days.

# Millet Crepes

Crepes, beloved in Brittany and a favorite Paris street food, are usually off-limits to those looking to avoid gluten. These, made with chia seeds and eggs, are a little sturdier than traditional buckwheat crepes, but they still have a delicate flavor. Serve plain, or fill with butter and jam for a morning treat. I've even used these in place of tortillas for tacos.

MAKES FOUR 7½-INCH (19-CM) CREPES

2 tablespoons (1 ounce; 28 g) unsalted butter

90 g (¾ cup) millet

1 tablespoon (12 g) chia seeds

2 large eggs

1 cup (240 ml) whole milk

¼ cup (60 ml) extra-virgin olive oil

In an 8-inch (20-cm) nonstick skillet, cook the butter over medium heat, stirring occasionally, until it browns and smells fragrant and toasted, about 5 minutes. Transfer to a small bowl and let cool. (Set the skillet aside; no need to wash it.)

In a food processor, pulse the millet and chia seeds until finely ground. Transfer to a large bowl and, using a fork, whisk in the eggs one at a time. Add 2 tablespoons (15 ml) of the milk and whisk to combine. Pour in the remaining milk and the browned butter and, using a handheld mixer or a whisk, mix until combined. Set aside at room temperature for 30 to 45 minutes, so the flour fully absorbs the liquid.

When you're ready to cook the crepes, heat the skillet you used to brown the butter over medium heat. Add 1 tablespoon (15 ml) of the olive oil and heat until warmed through. Pour one-quarter of the batter into the pan and cook until the edges of the crepe start to shrink slightly from the sides of the pan, 1 to 2 minutes; when you lift up an edge, the bottom should be golden. Using a spatula, flip the crepe and cook until golden on the other side and cooked through, 1 to 2 minutes. Transfer to a plate and repeat with the remaining oil and batter, stacking the crepes. Serve warm.

# Millet Polenta with Crisp Mushrooms

Until recently, millet hasn't been embraced much in Europe (that is, unless you count its role in bird feed). So I'm happy to see millet becoming more available in stores in France. It has a lovely mild, almost sweet, flavor. Now that I've discovered this grain's versatility, I don't want to share it with the birds! Here I use it in polenta in place of cornmeal; the result is a little more floral with a lighter texture.

Cheese and a mushroom topping heighten the grain's earthy undertones. You can serve the polenta at room temperature or slice it and panfry.

SERVES 4

### FOR THE POLENTA

1 tablespoon (½ ounce; 14 g) unsalted butter, softened, for the baking dish

¾ cup (150 g) millet

1¾ cups (420 ml) water

1 teaspoon (6 g) fine sea salt, or more to taste

½ cup (55 g) freshly grated Parmigiano-Reggiano

1 tablespoon (15 ml) fresh lemon juice, or more to taste

### FOR THE MUSHROOMS

2 tablespoons (30 ml) extra-virgin olive oil

12 ounces (340 g) maitake mushrooms, cut into 1-inch (2.5-cm) pieces

Fine sea salt and freshly ground black pepper

3 tablespoons (1½ ounces; 42 g) unsalted butter

2 fresh thyme sprigs

1 fresh rosemary sprig

Olive oil or salted butter, for searing (optional)

**MAKE THE POLENTA:** Butter an 8-inch (20-cm) round baking dish and set aside.

In a medium skillet, toast the millet over medium heat, stirring often, until it starts to smell toasty (almost like popcorn), about 5 minutes. Add the water and salt and stir to combine. Cook, stirring often, until the millet absorbs most of the water, 10 to 15 minutes.

Stir in the cheese in 3 additions until combined, and continue to cook, stirring often, until the millet is tender, 15 to 20 minutes more; add more water if it evaporates before the millet is done. Remove the pan from the heat and stir in the lemon juice. Season to taste with additional salt and juice if necessary.

Pour the polenta into the baking dish and smooth the top with a spatula. Let cool, then cover with plastic wrap and refrigerate until chilled and set, at least 2 hours, and up to overnight. (Bring to room temperature before serving.)

**MAKE THE MUSHROOMS:** Line a plate with paper towels. Heat the oil in a large skillet over high heat. Add the mushrooms and sear until the first side is golden brown, 3 to 4 minutes. Season with salt and pepper, stir, and cook, stirring occasionally, until the mushrooms are golden brown on all sides and crisp, 4 to 5 minutes more.

Reduce the heat to medium and add the butter, thyme, and rosemary. Cook, stirring often to baste the mushrooms with the butter, until the butter begins to brown and the mushrooms are tender. Transfer to the paper towel–lined plate. Remove and discard the herb sprigs.

To serve, slice the polenta into wedges and top with the mushrooms. Alternatively, heat a little olive oil or salted butter in a skillet and sear the polenta wedges until warmed through, then top with the mushrooms.

# Sources

### POILÂNE

You can order breads, cookies, and other treats, as well as our flour and items like bread bags, bread knives, and proofing baskets, directly from Poilâne.

**poilane.com**

We ship to wherever FedEx delivers.

### BEE POLLEN

**glorybee.com**

### BLACK GARLIC

**blackgarlicna.com**

### CHOCOLATE

We use chocolate from Michel Cluizel.

**cluizel.us**

### CHRISTINE FERBER JAMS AND JELLIES

An extraordinary pastry chef renowned for her jams.

**goldbelly.com**

### KING ARTHUR FLOUR

Sells a variety of flours.

**kingarthurflour.com**

### LINEN BREAD BAGS

If you're crafty, you can easily make a linen bag. We sell one on poilane.com that is large enough to hold our signature sourdough. Other sources:

**marchsf.com**
**lakeshorelinen.com**

### MAPLE CRUNCHIES/SPRINKLES

**iokavalleyfarm.com**
**greenmountaingoodness.com**

### SPICES

Olivier Roellinger, a three-Michelin-star French chef and owner of Épices Roellinger, makes the black pepper blend, Poivre des Mondes, that we use in our pain de mie. To find his pepper online, search for "Peppers of the World" on the list. He also makes Poudre Kawa for our Cardamom-Ginger–Swirled Brioche Feuilletée. The company sells licorice powder, too. Roellinger has several stores in France, each a stunning boutique of hand-selected spices and blends from around the world.

**epices-roellinger.com**

You can find Apollonia N.29 Spice Blend for Spice Cake at Lior Lev Sercarz's New York City–based La Boîte.

**laboiteny.com**

# Index